Wow, You Look Terrible!

HOW TO PARENT LESS AND LIVE MORE

Danny Ricker

FOREWORD BY
Jimmy Kimmel

HYPERION AVENUE
LOS ANGELES   NEW YORK

First Edition, April 2025
10 9 8 7 6 5 4 3 2 1
FAC-004510-25037
Printed in the United States of America

This book is set in Bookmania, Futura, and Chronicle
Book design by Amy C. King
Illustrations by Jon Kutt
Illustrations © Disney Enterprises, Inc.
Photos on pages 24, 28, 115, 133, 152, 154, 155, 158, 167, 193, 211, 217, 226, 239
courtesy of author
Photos on pages 17, 19, 20, 30, 35, 53, 59, 60, 95, 96, 118, 121, 141, 148, 149, 160,
176, 185, 188, 194, 198, 202, 206, 207 © Adobe Stock

Library of Congress Control Number: 2024940485
ISBN 978-1-368-11091-4
Reinforced binding

www.HyperionAvenueBooks.com

SUSTAINABLE FORESTRY INITIATIVE

Certified Sourcing

www.forests.org
SFI-01681

Logo Applies to Text Stock Only

FOR KELLY, CAP, AND BINGO

Contents

PART III: YOUR MIND

Foreword

As part of our daily writing assignment, to encourage random thoughts, I ask our staff writers to include what we call "observations." These are thoughts unrelated to the news or events of the day and, as they are not required, fall into the extra-credit category. Danny Ricker is an extra-credit kind of guy. He and his wife wear identical eyeglasses, he rides a Vespa to the office (always with helmet tightly secured) and loves Spider-Man, *Star Wars*, and '90s ska. Danny has a lot of checkered shirts and, while I've never been invited to his home (another reason I like him), I am confident that it is as neat and clean as he is.

To no one's surprise, Danny had one girlfriend and married her. Once he and Kelly tied the knot, his single-guy observations about Peter Parker and scooters gave way to thoughts like this . . .

Getting married to someone is basically saying "I agree to have in-depth conversations about decorative pillows with you."

A few years later, Danny and Kelly had a daughter, followed

by a son, and he began writing about the children almost exclusively. . . .

> *Rough morning in our house. Just had to explain*
> *to my daughter that alligators are real.*

And . . .

> *What's it like to be a parent? I just had to stop*
> *working so I could wipe the ass of someone who*
> *was, at full volume, singing "Silver and Gold" from*
> Rudolph the Red-Nosed Reindeer *(It's July).*

New-Dad Danny's musings were amusing, but of no use to me or our show. I suggested he might want to put them in a book to help other ridiculous parents feel less alone. Another reason I like Danny is because he is one of only two or three people on Earth who listen to me. At home, I often wonder if my voice is audible. After being ignored by my family three, four, sometimes up to eleven times in a row, I loudly say the words "CAN ANYONE HEAR ME? CAN ANYONE HEAR SOUND COMING OUT OF MY MOUTH?!"

But this guy Danny—I told him to write a book and he wrote one. Which, to be honest, makes me wonder how far I could take this. And now that he's written the book, you've either purchased, been gifted, or stolen it. "Hakuna matata! The circle of life!" (Like most guys who share eyeglasses with his wife, Danny is quick to teach others that "hakuna matata" translates to "no worries" and NOT "the circle of life." I added this to annoy him.)

Thank you for reading this book. If you have kids, I think you'll relate to and enjoy it as much as I did. If you don't have kids, let it serve as a warning. Most importantly, the fact that this book exists is more proof that I am always right.

Disingenuously,
Jimmy Kimmel

Introduction

HI. YOU DON'T SEEM WELL.

I can feel your hands trembling. Your eyes are sunken. There's Play-Doh in your jowls. The end of your rope has not only been reached; it is completely frayed and connected by just a single, quivering fiber. It's 3 a.m., and as you bounce a baby on your knee while cry-singing the alphabet, you can't help but wonder what the hell just happened to you. Before kids you were a carefree twentysomething with a packed travel schedule and a nontraditional haircut. You had a career and hobbies, clothes that both fit and didn't have wads of taffy in the pockets. Oh yeah and sex. You had that too.

But now in those terrifying moments when you catch your reflection in the side mirror of your ridiculous minivan, you no longer see that person. You don't even see *a* person. You see a parent. At some point after having children you went through a metamorphosis, but instead of becoming a butterfly, you turned into a boring, fatter, lonelier husk of your former self with stress-induced eczema and a hump in your back. You love being a parent, but is that all you are now? Is your sole purpose in this life to microwave pigs in a fucking blanket? The answer is no. The old you . . . the *real* you . . . is still buried deep inside under an avalanche of diaper creams and Barbie debris, and I'm here to pull that lost soul back into the light.

My name is Danny Ricker. While I am a comedy writer by trade, I am also a parent who has spent the last ten years raising two small children. During that harrowing decade I have done it all: I've potty trained a toddler during a pandemic. I've fallen out of a tree while rescuing a toy airplane. I've "cured a headache" by surgically removing a piece of bagel from my child's nose. I've stepped barefoot in my son's barf, which my son found quite delightful.

And despite all that, being a parent is the best part of my life. My kids are my two favorite people. But I gradually began to realize that the more I became their parent, the less I became myself. I was not a fully formed adult who happened to have children. I was my kids' service animal. For thirty years I was Batman, then one day I woke up an Alfred. So I set out to change that, not just for me, but for parents all around the world.

Parenting by its nature is a fundamentally absurd process and there's nothing we can do about a lot of it. Our children whine, they teethe, they use our most expensive collectible to smash our most cherished heirloom, and it's been that way since the dawn of humanity. Even cave parents shared knowing glances that said, "What the *fuck* is up with *Grog*?"

But I believe the hardest aspects of raising kids are the Sisyphean terrors we inflict upon ourselves. Even though parents are infinitely exhausted, at every turn we willingly *amplify* our children's insanity thousands of times over: We spend fortunes on elaborate birthday parties our kids will neither remember nor appreciate. We engage in bedtime routines that are longer than the runtime of *The Godfather Part II*.

We put elves on our shelves, like a bunch of damn fools. And *that* is when we lose ourselves.

Look, our kids deserve love, safety, respect, and a childhood filled with wonder.

HOWEVER.

As parents we deserve a few things too: a social life, expendable income, and the right to shower without a kid kicking the door in to tell us that he saw a bug. So how do we meet our children in the middle? How do we ensure they are physically and emotionally nurtured while ensuring *we* don't spend our lives as their unpaid interns? The answer is to strip the nonsense out of parenting and claw our personal lives back inch by fucking inch.

Just like Stella, I'm on a quest to get our collective groove back. For years now, I have been painstakingly examining the parenting process, searching for the secret nooks and crannies where we can regain some ground. Using that research, I've developed an intricate parent productivity system built on real-world experience, bounce house workouts, recipes, equations, inventions, flowcharts, schemes, grifts, meditations, hallucinations, places to hide, excuses to drink, fictional characters, and highly effective lies that will have no negative impact on your kids but add immeasurable value back to your life.

You are holding in your hands the Fruit by the Foot of my labors, and over the course of this book I will make you whole again by eliminating self-imposed preposterousness from your parenting in three major areas.

YOUR TIME

If you let them, your kids will consume every second of it, probably telling you about submarines or beavers or some thrilling story not even *they* know the ending to. I will teach you to whittle this obstruction out of your child-rearing to reclaim the one thing no parent is given: free time.

YOUR MONEY

Having kids is a terrible financial investment. It begins with thousands of dollars in medical bills to birth them, and ends with *hundreds* of thousands in college tuition. Even if they do eventually get a job, they spend all their earnings doing drugs at Coachella. I'll show you how to recoup those sunken costs by cutting all unnecessary prepubescent line items out of your budget.

YOUR MIND

Your children surround you in a vortex of lunacy. It swirls so frantically that if you don't batten down your mental hatches, your sanity will be thrown overboard and lost at sea for good. I will explore the most common ways kids warp our reality and demonstrate how to come out the other side with most of your marbles intact.

This journey will take sacrifice. If you follow my teachings, your children will not remember you as a fun person, but that's the point. "Fun" people become professional puppeteers or Instagram hot sauce influencers or medical device salesmen with thinly veiled drinking problems. You are a parent now, and if you're going to get through this while maintaining your sense of self, you need to approach the task using a cold, precision engineering typically reserved for German cars. Adopting my extreme form of efficiency will not be easy, but I promise you this: Being a parent and having a life are not mutually exclusive activities. So get down off that ledge and take my hand. It's time for you . . . for me . . . for *all* of us . . . to parent less and live more.

PART I

Your Time

The biggest complaint I hear from parents is that they no longer have time to do the things *they* want to do. However, I think that's the wrong way of looking at it, because while kids do ask for a lot of your time, not all those asks are of equal importance. Being a parent to young children is like being a personal assistant to Kanye West, and you need to sort through which of their demands actually require the attention of a human adult. "Yes, I can make you breakfast. No, we cannot fly to space in a hot air balloon."

You should think of your list of daily parental duties as a bag of chips at the gas station. From the outside, it looks like it's so full of Fritos it's going to explode. But when you open it up? Really only the bottom third of that bag is of any real substance. Those fifteen broken corn chips represent the things you *actually* need to do as a parent: feeding, schooling, making fart sounds in the crooks of their sweaty little elbows, etcetera. The upper two thirds of the bag are abject nothingness. They're for show. They represent all the unnecessary stuff we do for our kids because we believe it'll make us "good" parents:

hand-sewing Halloween costumes, singing lengthy "goodnight songs" to a stuffed seal, and settling inter-sibling quarrels over whether belly buttons are "the opposite of nipples."

So how are we going to reclaim the remaining salty carbohydrate mist in that bag for ourselves? By taking a sober look at every request of our time and saying no to the ones that aren't absolutely critical to the well-being of our children. We'll also save time by distilling each act of parenting down to its most molecular form, trimming away the fat to get our day back a few precious seconds at a time. And finally, we'll redefine what "personal time" means to us, so recreational activities can be done in tandem with seemingly opposing chores. Kinda like how for many years Jason Momoa found a way to consume nothing but Guinness stout while retaining the title of "Hollywood's Most Fuckable Fish."

They say freedom isn't free. And for parents, neither is free time. So let's dig in and fight for what's ours. ("Ours" being the occasional chance to have fun for one minute, one time, once a year.)

THE 17-MINUTE BIRTHDAY PARTY

There are few parenting processes more time-consuming than throwing your child a birthday party. You dedicate weeks to sending out invites, decorating the house, and procuring enough refined sugar to kill a water buffalo. Then on the day, you're required to spend hours showing a mob of rabid second-graders the time of their lives while also preventing them from sharpening sticks, forming hunting tribes, and devolving into a full-blown *Lord of the Flies* situation. But it doesn't have to be this way.

I've designed a plan that gives your child everything they want out of a birthday while drastically reducing your total time investment. Technically speaking, this *is* a party, but it more closely resembles a military strike so ruthlessly efficient it would make Napoleon Bonaparte shit his cute lil' knickers. Here is a step-by-step guide to celebrating the birth of your child in just seventeen minutes (and not a second more).

10:00 A.M.–10:03 A.M.: ARRIVALS

All party attendees must be lined up and ready by 10 a.m. sharp. You and your child will stand at the entryway of your home to receive the guests, and over the next 180 seconds each invitee will march inside to present their gift offering to the birthday boy or girl. (These should be *unwrapped*, as eliminating the present-opening process can shave a good half hour off any

party.) Small talk is not only discouraged at this juncture, but strictly prohibited. Admission will be cut off at exactly the three-minute mark because this party is like a Southwest flight: If you're not there before the door closes? Tough titties, try again next year.

10:03 A.M.–10:04 A.M.: QUICKIE CLOWN

Time for some entertainment! Immediately corral the children around the clinically depressed party clown you hired off Craigslist. His name is Banjo and this is not how he expected his life to turn out, which is good because that means he wants to get this over with even faster than you do. Banjo will do no more than one party trick, and that's probably for the best considering how much he reeks of bourbon. Quickly usher the kids outside with their disappointing balloon animals (all of which are "a log"), then dismiss Banjo to go sigh loudly in his 2003 Honda CR-V.

10:04 A.M.–10:07 A.M.: PIN THE TAIL ON THE DONKEY ("NO BLINDFOLD" EDITION)

You are obligated to include at least one game at your child's party, but nowhere in the rule book does it say it needs to be difficult. Tape a picture of a donkey to the wall, hand each kid a tail, and tell them to go for it. No blindfold, no spinning. Just let all twenty-five kids walk up and place the tail in the exact right spot. If a child complains the game is boring, remind Hudson (his name is always Hudson) that there's really a ceiling on how fun a game involving a picture of a donkey can be, then 86 that little ingrate from the party. His toxic masculinity was only going to slow things down. Now that everyone (minus *Hudson*) has won the game, they've qualified to participate in the main event: the motherfuckin' CAKE JUMP.

10:07 A.M.–10:13 A.M.: THE MOTHERFUCKIN' CAKE JUMP

This stage combines two classic kid party activities (eating pastries and Zone 5 cardio), conducting them simultaneously for maximum time savings. Briskly trot all the children to an awaiting bouncy castle, where they will begin to jump around wildly and give each other festive head trauma. There will be crying almost immediately, which is when you'll hurl a sheet cake into the center of the castle (candles unlit!) and let them tear it apart like a swarm of Black Friday shoppers fighting over a two-dollar panini press. While the cake is usually reserved as the grand finale of a party, you need to serve it now because the next stage strategically uses the sugar rush the kids just got from mainlining buttercream frosting.

10:13 A.M.–10:15 A.M.: PIÑATA EXPLOSIVO

The piñata portion of a children's party is always painfully long because their little noodle arms aren't yet strong enough to puncture a papier-mâché unicorn. But thanks to the high-octane mix of bounce house adrenaline and cake batter coursing through their nervous systems, they should tear through that bitch like Jose Canseco on a steroid bender. If they are still unable to break open the piñata though, call Banjo back in to finish the job. (While his arms are weak from the depression, his heart is filled with rage.) Let the kids eat as much floor candy as possible to make sure they get enough exit velocity to vacate the premises.

10:16 A.M.: WARNING BLAST

Blow an air horn to inform your guests the time has come to get the fuck off your property.

10:17 A.M.: EVACUATE

Unplug the bounce house motor (if there are any kids trapped inside, it's their fault for not heeding the warning blast) and hastily sing "Happy Birthday" as you shoo everyone out of your home. Most of the children will scatter like subway rats, but remember to check all your cabinets, crawl spaces, and air ducts for any kids who might have crawled inside to ride out a Twizzlers overdose. Once the house is clear, give Banjo his fifty bucks and a long hug, letting him know things are tough but he is loved. Shut the door, and as your child slips into a euphoric birthday coma, enjoy the extra six hours you've just added to your Saturday like the goddamn hero you are.

THROW AWAY THEIR STUFF

When you cohabitate with kids, your home becomes overrun with two types of items: Things and Stuff. *Things* are objects you need to raise your children, like cribs, bottles, high chairs, what have you. The real threat to your time is *Stuff*.

Stuff can often masquerade as Things, but it is actually a by-product of them: a discharge of sorts. When you are tidying up at night, you might grab a handful of Stuff that consists of a Barbie shoe, a piece of a puzzle, a picture your kid drew of a flamingo driving a tractor, and a crushed-up Dasani bottle. Now, you *could* spend the rest of your evening searching for a shoeless Barbie, finding the other 199 pieces of that puzzle, framing the picture of the tractor flamingo (which honestly looks more like a shrimp in a Jeep), and arguing with a toddler over whether the flattened water bottle is, in fact, a flute. Or you *could* just ... throw all that shit away.

Believe me when I say that throwing away Stuff while your kids aren't looking doesn't just save you time—it is one of the great joys of parenting. I love it. I experience it like the scene from *Titanic* where the old lady drops the necklace into the ocean: in slow motion while a Celine Dion song swells in my heart. When your house is a disaster, just pick up a loose hand-ful of Stuff, shake it in your hand like you're rolling dice at the craps table, and wing it so hard into the trash that you break the sound barrier. YOU WILL FEEL ALIVE.

I can already hear some of you eco-warriors saying this is wasteful, that it'd be better to find a new owner for these items instead of scrapping them. And you know, maybe you're right.

So I'm going to drive over to your house right now and drop off some of the Stuff that's built up in my own home. I hope you enjoy your new...

...dinosaur with a broken arm, bowling ball whose pins were immediately lost, and chair the size of an Advil. It will pair nicely with this Showcase Showdown collection of...

...glow sticks that no longer glow, a skateboard for a mouse, a sock with no mate, a Marshall slipper (also with no mate), a #2 block, and three nondescript pieces of plastic. And you know what I think is going to really complement your living room?

This plate filled with punched paper holes on your TV stand. Really ties the whole room together! Oh, what's that? You want to chuck this bullshit in a dumpster too? Something told me you'd come around.

But there is a catch here. While hurtling your kids' Stuff into the trash is both effective and deeply satisfying, they will be inconsolable if they see you dispose of even a single piece of their treasured garbage. Like newborn ducklings, children imprint on every piece of junk they've ever touched and become bonded to it for life, so discretion is of the utmost importance here. You must put meticulous planning into where and how you dispose of Stuff—like a cross between Marie Kondo and the Zodiac Killer—and you can do so using my Three Surefire Tips for Successful Stuff Removal.

TIP #1: WORK UNDER THE CLOAK OF DARKNESS

Because your kids are so emotionally connected to their Stuff, you can only safely throw it away while they're asleep. Many years ago I tried to institute a policy in my home where any toys not picked up by bedtime would be thrown away by the "Trash Man." The Trash Man was me, walking around the house with a garbage bag yelling, "I am the Trash Man!" Unfortunately, this made my kids start crying immediately, and the character was sent into early retirement. But this level of theatrics is unnecessary. As you walk around the house before bed, just silently earmark which piles of your child's most cherished litter will be out on the curb by nightfall.

TIP #2: COVER YOUR TRACKS

Stuff should only be disposed of in outdoor bins that are too tall for your children to open. However, if you must dispose of Stuff inside, place a layer of BT (Boring Trash™) on top of it— anything from asparagus clippings to that jury duty summons you're pretending you never got. BT will usually throw kids off the trail, which is important because even if you're an Academy Award–winning actor, if you hear the phrase

"Mommy? Why is my egg carton spaceship in the *trash*?!" you are fucked.

TIP #3: USE THE PURGATORY CABINET

The Purgatory Cabinet is one of my greatest creations, and I hope this doesn't sound arrogant, but I consider it a crime that I've yet to receive a Nobel Prize for its groundbreaking contributions to the institution of parenting. The Purgatory Cabinet is simply that, a cabinet, where I place Stuff I'd like to get rid of but fear my children will notice its absence and cause a whole fucking thing. The way it works is, I hide an item in this cabinet for one week, and if my kids don't ask about it during that time, it has completed its transformation from Stuff to trash and is off to the dump. But! If my kids come to me with tears in their eyes, saying they can't find their beloved toilet paper tube (or whatever), why . . . I had just put it in this cabinet for safekeeping, like the caring, thoughtful parent I am!

My wife and I have employed our Purgatory Cabinet many times to great success. For instance, our family used to have a "Special Spoon," which was not *actually* special, of course. It was just an oyster spoon a weird uncle gave us from our wedding registry, but the kids had decided this was the Rolls-Royce of flatware and fought over it constantly. Food tasted better off this thing, it was a status symbol in our breakfast nook, and the cause of most predawn bawling in our home. But one day I was unloading it from the dishwasher, and instead of going back into the silverware drawer, the Special Spoon made an unscheduled stop in the Purgatory Cabinet. It stayed there for seven luxurious nights before making a connecting flight to our local Goodwill, which created peace in our home and gave a major glow-up to an amateur oyster enthusiast in our community.

This magic cabinet also saved us the time a masochistic parent put *fucking whistles* in the goodie bags at a birthday party our son attended. It is not an exaggeration to say that my five-year-old wielding this small piece of plastic made our lives one bajillion times worse. But thanks to the Purgatory Cabinet, I didn't need to spend time tying the whistle around a brick and throwing it back through that parent's window.

However, our most perilous experience with the Purgatory Cabinet was actually the one that created it. My grandmother had gifted us some vintage children's books she still had from when she was a little girl, one of which was a "classic" our daughter fell in love with and wanted to read multiple times a day. Unfortunately, the title of that book was *The Five Chinese Brothers.*

In the name of taste, I will not reprint the book's cover image here. Just know that if an artist drew it today, they'd be loaded into a cannon and fired into the sun. And yet! The inside of the book was somehow even more problematic than the outside. This is literally the opening line:

> *"Once upon a time there were Five Chinese Brothers*
> *and they all looked exactly alike."*
> —*From* **The Five Chinese Brothers** *(NOT ME.)*

While I'm sure the (Swiss!) author meant well when she published this in 1938, eighty years had passed, and we didn't *love* the taste of that sentence in our mouths. Plus the plot of this book involves some townspeople trying to violently murder the Five Chinese Brothers by setting them on fire, throwing them in the ocean, cooking them in an oven, and publicly beheading them, all because the first Chinese Brother fucking *drowned* a kid.... *Nighty night, sweetheart!*

So the Purgatory Cabinet was forged, where *The Five Chinese Brothers* bunked up for a week. Unbeknownst to our daughter, the book was then sent to a Los Angeles landfill, where it will be discovered centuries from now by horrified anthropologists.

You no longer need to waste your days shuffling around the house like a resentful Roomba. It is time to excuse yourself from mankind's least rewarding scavenger hunt. Throw away your kids' Stuff. Do it proudly. Do it often. Do it quietly. Do it hard. And don't spend your precious time figuring out where to put ... this.

THE HOUDINI METHOD

In my most frazzled moments as a parent, and I swear this is true, I fantasize about being hospitalized. Nothing serious, maybe just a bout of appendicitis where I can spend a couple guilt-free days sitting in silence and reading a book that doesn't have little cardboard flaps in it. Or better yet: serving a six-month jail sentence for a white-collar crime I didn't commit. Eventually I'll be exonerated, and in the meantime enjoy some sloppy joes and tight-knit gang associations that'll last a lifetime.

We all just need a break sometimes, and unfortunately kids are the only bosses who aren't required to give you a state-mandated fifteen minutes to vape. So how do we, against infinite resistance, carve out time to be alone? Like the great Harry Houdini, we must learn to vanish.

But hiding from kids is much harder than you'd think. All those classic moves like "I'm Going to the Bathroom" or "I'm on the Phone" *would* work if our children had any respect for our privacy, but since they don't, we'll need to go deep undercover. And to do that we're going to learn from the dumbest humans on planet Earth: people who do social media challenges.

For the uninitiated, social media challenges are online dares performed by irritating twentysomethings and unemployable thirtysomethings who post videos of themselves doing a variety of regrettable activities. These usually involve such scholarly pursuits as eating Tide Pods and snorting condoms, but in 2016 there was a popular one called the "24 Hour Fort Challenge" where people hid in stores just before closing with the goal of staying in the building overnight without getting caught. They accomplished this by building "forts" out of the store's products, crouching behind stacks of toilet paper, and crawling inside furniture at major retailers like Ikea, Walmart, and Costco. While this was dangerous, illegal, and (I cannot stress this enough) annoying, there is an important lesson we can glean from these idiots: *Any* spot can be a hiding spot if you are both physically and morally flexible. Standing on the shoulders of these dipshits, I've created this series of parental concealment methods guaranteed to net you a few moments to lie down on the lowdown.

"BOX HER UP!"

The next time you purchase a large appliance, keep the box it was shipped in. Then gradually over a few months, use that box to "store" some "random" items, including pillows, nonperishable food, a 32″ television, and a bedpan. While most childless adults would bristle at the idea of spending a few hours crammed inside the packing materials of a Samsung dishwasher, to you this will feel like the first-class cabin on a transatlantic flight. So crack open a can of corn, turn on the Hallmark Channel, and take a deep breath that has a *little* too much carbon dioxide because you forgot to poke air holes.

THE HIDE-AND-SEEK CONUNDRUM

The game Hide-and-Seek has been around for over two thousand years, and yet parents have never figured out how to use it to their advantage. I've finally cracked this nut though, and all you have to do is exploit a loophole where the rules of the game bump up against child endangerment laws. If my kids want me to play Hide-and-Seek when I'm feeling spent, I quickly agree and offer to be the first hider. As soon as they close their eyes to count, I bolt out to the front yard and crouch behind a bush. Now, my kids aren't allowed to go in the front yard unless I'm with them, but at this point they don't *know* if I'm in the front yard, and they can't come out to *look* for me without ... me. This is the "Cayman Islands bank account" of hiding spots and it works like a charm. You'll have at least ten minutes of solitude, and if your neighbor asks why you're squatting in the hedges watching tennis highlights on an iPad, you tell Todd to mind his own fucking business.

THE SERENITY SNORKEL

Cartoons from the 1930s didn't set the best example for kids (mostly because they starred racist animals who shoved dynamite down people's pants), but they did create a trope we can use to get ourselves a little parental enchantment under the sea. Imagine, if you will, a cartoon bear getting chased by a swarm of angry bees, and as that little fella runs for his life, he sees a lake. What does he do? He dives *into* that lake, and breathes through a straw until the bees fly on by. In many metaphorical ways, you are that bear and your kids are those bees, so let's get you a straw. Every hardware store sells ten-foot PVC pipes for less than five bucks, a small investment that will allow you to breathe comfortably at the bottom of your pool, Jacuzzi, or local reservoir. Once your kids lose interest in finding you and the coast is clear, you're free to use your twenty thousand leagues of free time however you wish. Most modern smartphones can be submerged for up to thirty minutes, which experts say is just enough time to enjoy an underwater rerun of *Young Sheldon*. Or put that sucker in a sandwich bag and binge-watch until Young Sheldon matures into Regular, Off-Putting Sheldon.

MOM-STER UNDER THE BED

The most common personal time our kids rob us of is that high-value real estate between when *they* go to bed and when *we* go to bed. They always need one more hug, one more sip of water, one more grisly detail of the *Dateline* murder-thon we're trying to watch. So if you're going to get that brief but important chunk of nighttime solace, you have to do it in a place your children would never dare look. And I know you've probably spent the majority of your kids' formative years trying to convince them there's *not* a demonic, child-eating beast that lives beneath their bed, but not so fast! Because if you play your cards right, their deep-seated fear of being devoured by a sub-mattress Demogorgon can be parlayed into a rather peaceful evening for you. Just before your little one goes down for the night, wedge yourself under their race-car bed. As soon as the lights go off, let out a satanic hiss, then bellow the phrase "Now it is time for the Feast of Souls!" This simple line of dialogue will strategically petrify your child, and just like a petrified piece of wood, they will sit perfectly still for hours and not pester you for Totino's Pizza Rolls.

VERTI-GO AWAY

When things get too hectic in your home, walk outside and climb the tallest tree you can find. You likely have not scaled a tree since you were seven years old, so this will be surprisingly difficult. You will both look and feel like a gorilla on Ambien, but keep going, because freedom is just a few branches away. Once you're up there, shout down to your children that you have an intense fear of heights, which you guess you forgot to mention to them until this very moment. Say you don't have the courage to shimmy down just yet, but that you might be relaxed enough to consider it after you finally read that romance novel you've been trying to finish all summer (the one about the emotionally distant naval officer with a bulge like Jon Hamm in Hawaiian shorts), which you just so happen to have tucked into your back pocket right now! Should they call the fire department to get you down? No.... No need to bother them. Unless those firemen happen to be emotionally distant or packin' Hamm.

LAUNDRY DAY LAY-LOW

This requires a sewing machine and the ability to slow your heart rate to forty beats per minute, but it's well worth it. You know those dirty clothes you've been asking your kids to pick up off the floor since the Obama administration? Grab a pile of them, stitch them together into a big messy bundle, and attach them to your arms and legs like so:

Then pop in those AirPods, put on your favorite podcast (one of those long ones where two NPResque ladies stretch a missing person's case out for three seasons before ultimately deciding "We may never know the truth"), and lie perfectly still for anywhere from one hour to one year. You'll be completely invisible, and the best part is you've now set a type of trap called a "honeypot," where the only way for your kids to find you is if they finally put away their goddamn laundry. *Checkmate.*

Are these methods extreme? Some of the more weak-minded parents out there might think so, but you're of sturdier stock. Your goal should be to hide so well that when you *are* eventually located, your kids will have to drag you out of a hole in the ground like when they found Saddam Hussein. You'll be hairy, emaciated, covered in soot, but you will have a smile on your face because you were finally able to catch up on every season of *RuPaul's Drag Race* (even the underwhelming European ones!).

THE BATH-TIME FLOWCHART

Johnson & Johnson commercials would have you believe that bathing your kids is a sacred act: a time when parent and child can relax and bond at the end of a long day before cozying up in their jam-jams and drifting off to sleep. This is dangerous propaganda.

Cleaning your children can be one of the most time-consuming processes you endure as a parent. It starts with begging them to get into the tub, followed by contentious negotiations over water temperature and which toys are considered submersible . . . then you wash their hair while they cry, then you wash their hair while *you* cry. Suddenly it's ninety minutes later, you're soaking wet, and all you've accomplished is scrubbing a little Sharpie off a human the size of a butternut squash.

Or maybe your kid loves the bath *too* much and would play in there all night, so bathing them is basically like asking, "Hey, before you go to bed would you like to take a trip to Six Flags Hurricane Harbor?"

But here's a little secret: You don't need to wash your kids every night. You may not even need to do it every *week*. Children have a base level of grime that is both natural and socially acceptable (similar to alpacas at the petting zoo). And while you should always bathe them when they truly need it, that occurrence happens much less often than the mainstream hygiene media would have you believe. Don't be a pawn in Big Shampoo's game. Let my Bath-Time Flowchart be your guide.

Do I Have To Bathe My Kid Tonight?

START → WHEN I SNIFF THEM, DO I RECOIL?

YES — AND I CAN KINDA TASTE THE SMELL

NO

BATH! (ugh) ← **NO** — CAN THE HOSE FIX THIS?

YES

NO — CLIMATE CHANGE HAS TRANSFORMED MY TOWN INTO A BARREN POSTAPOCALYPTIC WASTELAND WHERE THE REMAINING FRESH WATER WE DO HAVE IS USED AS A FORM OF CURRENCY

COULD I DO THAT THING I DO WITH MY CAR WHERE I JUST WAIT FOR IT TO RAIN?

YES →

NO

YES — CONFIRMED BY THE CDC

OH GOD, IS THAT MOLD? →

MAYBE

YES

BECAUSE MY CHILD IS NOT HIGH ON PEYOTE AND PLAYING A DRUM

NO — WILL ANYONE BELIEVE ME IF I SAY MY CHILD JUST SPENT THE WEEKEND AT BURNING MAN?

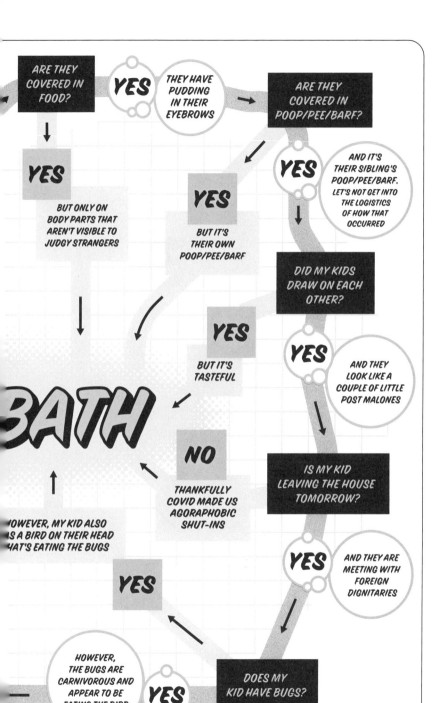

NO PROMISES MADE, NO PROMISES KEPT

There are three things in life you should never do under any circumstances: Use a Groupon for dental surgery, criticize Taylor Swift on the internet, and make a promise to your child.

That's because kids are human sponges, anthropomorphic tape recorders, miniature trial lawyers who can't remember to not touch the stove—but *can* recall every word you've ever said and fuckin' *nail* you on it. If you mention Monday morning that you *might* take them to McDonald's Sunday afternoon, there's no question that when the time comes you'll be eating McGriddles while your kids contract norovirus in a ball pit.

And there is no agreement more ironclad than telling a five-year-old you will be getting ice cream later that day. Your house could be burning down, and as you're kicking out a window to rescue your child from the approaching inferno, you will faintly hear: "**cough* *cough** Mommy? After we climb out this window **cough* *cough** are we going to Baskin-Robbins?" So we must be vigilant, for even the most casual of promises to a kid has the potential to consume massive amounts of our time. I have personal experience in this particular arena.

A few years ago, my daughter informed me that her friend had a crush on someone named Oscar. I assumed that was a boy from school, but it was actually an actor named Sean Michael Kyer, who played a *character* named Oscar on the TV show *Odd Squad*. My daughter, because she is a good person and bad at math, became obsessed with making enough money to buy her friend a plane ticket to go meet Oscar in person. This was not the most solid plan for a few reasons:

1. Plane tickets are extremely expensive.
2. Oscar is not real.
3. My daughter and her friend were seven, and at the time "Oscar" was in his early twenties.
4. When I asked my daughter where Oscar lives, she said, "I don't know, Canada?"

But I was blinded by a miscalculated desire to be an encouraging father, and it was in this moment I made a major tactical error: I said, "Sure! We can do that." And with those five simple words, my weekend was lost.

As soon as she had the green light, my daughter started brainstorming business ideas like a Silicon Valley tech bro on Adderall. "Maybe I can sell your old clothes! What about our furniture?!" I assumed she'd eventually lose interest in her fledgling start-up, but her determination only intensified. She then informed me she was going to raise the necessary travel funds by selling some of her old books in the front yard, and since children are very enticing to both kidnappers and mountain lions, you're not supposed to leave them unattended outside. That meant I was now intimately involved in this plot to get my daughter's friend into the arms of a fictional character from a 2014 PBS Kids show.

While I was impressed by both her dedication to her friend and her entrepreneurial spirit, this was also some bullshit. So I tried to politely suggest that maybe selling the eleven tattered books she'd curated wouldn't net us the $580 required to buy a coach seat to "I don't know, Canada?" but she would not take no for an answer. She made a sign, set up shop on the lawn, and there we sat. But then the worst possible thing happened: She immediately made a sale.

A little boy and his mom happened to be walking by and bought *two* of the books. We had two dollars toward that plane ticket (0.3 percent of the way there!) and my daughter now considered herself a Dr. Dre–level business mogul. So she put plans in motion to expand her empire into a second retail sector: rocks. When I tried to gently explain that our neighbors were probably not going to buy rocks from our yard, considering they had their own yards containing a number of free rocks, she told me I was being negative, and off we went.

We walked around our neighborhood pulling a wagon full of stones, unsuccessfully pitching our "Postmates for rocks" business like rejects from *Shark Tank*. And as the sun went down, we had a conversation about how sometimes life can disappoint us, and that even the best of intentions don't always lead to the results we want. Again, this was all so her *friend could meet an imaginary person.*

To help you avoid accidentally committing hours of your life to similar preschool pyramid schemes, I've generated a list of vague yet legally sound responses you can give your kids when they try to corner you into promising them something insane.

"MAYBE!"

In the self-help space, a lot of attention is given to the power of *yes*, but the most formidable word a parent can wield is *maybe*. While it's just five letters, *maybe* is an effective countermeasure because it *means* no, but it *feels* like yes.

"Can you fly your drone in church? Maybe!"

"Can you get a pet snake and keep it in the bathtub? Maybe!"

"Can you drive the car, even though you're two feet tall and only recently gained an understanding of object permanence? Maybe!"

Maybe can also put a quick stop to any line of questioning you're not prepared to answer. "Have I ever seen Dad naked? . . . Maybe!"

"WE'LL HAVE TO SEE"

"We'll have to see" is a great one because it implies that some sort of exploratory committee will be formed to investigate your child's request and issue a verdict in a detailed report. The reality, of course, is you have no intention of speaking of it ever again. "Can you have a chain saw for Christmas? We'll have to see what the Supreme Court decides."

"THAT SOUNDS FUN!"

Technically this is not a lie, because *everything* kids want to do sounds fun. Watch YouTube on a roller coaster? Pick up every single stick at the park and pretend it's a lightsaber? Capture a squirrel and teach it the alphabet? We're not doing *any* of that shit, but it *Does! Sound! Fun!*

"INTERESTING!"

This is also not a lie, because it *is* interesting that your child thinks you'd want to take them mini-golfing three days in a row.

"I HEAR YOU"

This lets kids know their ridiculous desires are understood, but conveniently leaves out the fact that you will not be considering their demands in the least.

"You want me to stop working so I can watch you count to a thousand. I *hear* you. And I *hear* that you want me to read you a Diary of a Wimpy Kid book, even though we literally just read that exact book cover to cover one second ago and you weren't paying attention. Believe me. I *hear* it."

If you get the intonation just right, they'll think you're about to say another sentence that will grant their wish, but it's actually just an ellipsis that goes on forever . . . . !

Remember: When you are talking to your kids, you are *always* on the record. Treat conversations with them like you're being deposed: Give noncommittal answers and have counsel present if possible. The stakes have never been higher, and one tiny misstep, even a single slip of the tongue, could see you serving five to eight weekend hours dressed as a knight at an elementary school Renaissance faire. Which, you know, *sounds fun!*

DO THE MATH

While much of raising children involves intuition passed down to us from the past three hundred generations of our species, most of those generations solved problems by beating each other on the head with rocks. But today we have evolved frontal lobes and iPhone calculators, so let's crunch some numbers. As a general rule of parenting, *everything* you do with children takes *much* longer than you anticipate. But exactly how much longer? And how are you supposed to plan any personal, non-kid recreation without this vital data?

That's exactly why I formulated and field-tested this batch of parenting equations. You'll now know the precise amount of time needed to get these tasks done, and be able to schedule in a little "you time" engaging in your favorite leisure activity: watching videos of sick skateboard tricks on YouTube. (I don't know you that well, but you definitely seem like the type of person who loves watching videos of sick skateboard tricks on YouTube.) Okay, pencils up, nerds, let's begin.

HOW LONG IT TAKES TO GET A FAMILY HOLIDAY PHOTO

Time for you and your spouse to get ready

✛

Time to comb kids' hair, which they have not done in the one year since you took your last holiday photo

✛

Time to change them into matching sweaters, which they claim are "so itchy it's *literally* killing" them

✛

Time to give up on the sweater pipe dream and let them wear what they want, which in this case is a *Minecraft* tank top the dog chewed a hole in

✛

Time for you and your spouse to get ready *again* because getting the kids ready gave you runny mascara and pit stains you could simply not bounce back from

✛

Time to set up the tripod on that nice grassy spot in the yard

✛

Time to find a new picture spot because the kids claim the grass is "so itchy it's *literally* killing" them

✛

Time to assemble your spouse, kids, and dog in one place, facing the same direction at the same moment. (However long you think this is going to take, multiply by fifty)

✛

Time to set the timer, run over to your family, take the

photo, check the photo, then notice the kids were not
smiling, looking at the camera, or even *in* the photo

✜

Time to repeat this process six hundred times

✜

Time to marvel at the fact that while your kids
haven't taken one good picture this entire time,
your dog is knocking this out of the fuckin' park

✜

Time to begin the bargaining process with your kids

✜

Time to get talked up to the deal: "If you kids
take one good photo, you will get a cupcake, an
extra hour of screens, and the opportunity to
punch me as hard as you can in the butt"

✜

Time to take one final photo, which is still terrible

✜

Time to get punched in the butt anyway

✜

Time to apply to community college

✜

Time to take an intensive six-week course on Photoshop

✜

Time to digitally alter the photo so it looks like your family
had literally one second of holiday harmony and peace

✜

Time to become an atheist so you
never have to do this again

HOW LONG IT TAKES TO "PLAY A STORY" WITH YOUR CHILD

Time to pick out the toys and designate which ones are "good guys" and "bad guys"

✚

Time to brainstorm the general plot

✚

Time for all your plot ideas to be rejected by your toddler, even though your grasp of story structure is *way* more advanced

✚

Time for your character to be defeated by an arsenal of previously unmentioned missiles, force fields, laser cannons, and attack robots

✚

Time for you to wrap up the story in a satisfying way

✚

Time for your child to introduce a new plot twist that, frankly, sullies the legacy of the story up until that point

✚

Time for you to wrap *that* story up in a satisfying way

✚

Time for your child to green-light a sequel to your story, which—hey, guess what?—is shooting right now

✚

Time for your child to develop this into an epic multi-movie franchise that even the producers of the Fast & Furious films would consider "a bit much"

✚

Time for you to finally get up after sitting on the
hardwood floor for two hours, which has caused
internal injuries you will carry to the grave

HOW LONG IT TAKES TO GO ON A
TRIP TO TARGET WITH YOUR CHILD

Time to drive to Target, during which you
explain to your child that the only thing
you'll be buying is dishwasher pods

✛

Time to load your child into the shopping
cart's bacteria-glazed foldout seat

✛

Time to curse the Target corporation for putting the area
where you strap your kids in *right* next to the Dollar Bin

✛

Time to remind your child that you're just there for
dishwasher pods, not bullshit from the Dollar Bin

✛

Time for your kid to pick out some bullshit from the
Dollar Bin, which somehow costs twenty-six dollars

✛

Time to chart a very circuitous route to the
dishwasher pod aisle, taking great care to not pass
any more items your kid might ask you for

✛

Time to accidentally turn down the candy aisle
and mouth *Shit!* at a display of Mike and Ikes

✛

Time to try to convince your kid that
Skittles are "too spicy" for them

✛

Time for that little charade to die on the vine

✛

Time for your child to talk you into buying
a bag of Skittles so large they'll probably set
some of them out in a bowl at your funeral

✛

Time to check out

✛

Time to drive home

✛

Time to realize you forgot to buy dishwasher pods

HOW LONG IT TAKES TO ANSWER A WORK EMAIL WHILE YOUR KIDS ARE HOME

Time to read your boss's email

✛

Time to type "Sorry for the delay" with one
hand while cleaning raspberry jam out of
your Blu-ray player with the other

✛

Time to come up with a response to your boss's query

✖

Number of random fucking questions your
child is asking you about clouds

—

Time it would take you to make your response
thoughtful, because you are also singing a song
about otters to stop your baby from crying

✣

Time to quickly type out a half-assed response
while half-assedly wiping your kid's ass

—

Time it would take to proofread the response, because
you really should have sent this email hours ago

✣

Time to hit Send

✣

Time to find new job, since you just got fired from
your current job, on account of the email

✣

Time for your kids to complain you work too much

HOW LONG IT TAKES TO GET YOUR
KID TO THE GATE AT THE AIRPORT

Time to unload your child's bags, which dwarf
your number of bags by a factor of four

✣

Time to check in for your flight while your
child kisses the ticket kiosk, giving her a
disease known as Influenza: Infinity

✣

Time to send your child through the metal detector

✛

Time to send your child through the metal detector again

✛

Time to send your child through the metal detector again

✛

Time to peek in her diaper, which is filled with pennies

✛

Time to send your child through the body scanner
instead, which is probably blasting her with tons of
radiation—but maybe it will cook off the kiosk Ebola?

✛

Time to walk halfway to the gate

✛

Time for your child to sob next to the host
station of a miniature Applebee's

✛

Time to walk the rest of the way to the gate

✛

Because she's "thirsty from crying," time
for your child to talk you into buying her a
lemonade that costs more than a tank of gas

✛

Time for you to come to terms with the
fact that you're going to need to take your
morning shit in this airport terminal

✛

Time to cram you, your child, and all your
luggage into a single bathroom stall

✛

Time for you to have the most horrifying bowel

movement of your life while you and your child
make haunting, unbroken eye contact

✤

Time to arrive at the gate just as they're letting
"families with young children" board first

✤

Time for all the childless passengers to give you dirty looks

✤

Time to strut past those haters 'cuz you don't give a FUCK

✤

Time to sit down in your seat, realize you
didn't bring your child's iPad, then get off the
plane and just drive home—not worth it

HOW LONG IT TAKES TO FIGURE OUT
WHICH MOVIE YOUR KID IS TALKING ABOUT

Time for kid to explain this movie is about a bear

✤

Time for you to guess *Kung Fu Panda*

✤

Time for your kid to say no, and also reject your guesses
of *Winnie the Pooh*, *Bad News Bears*, and *Cocaine Bear*

✤

Time for your kid to tell you that in this
movie, the bear shoots a gun

✤

Time for you to ask who the bear shoots the gun at

✤

Time for your kid to say "Some white people"

✛

Time for you to ask if this was actually
a dream your kid had

✛

Time for your kid to say no, they saw it on Disney+

✛

Time for your kid to say Santa Claus is in
the movie, and he goes to a restaurant

✛

Time for you to wonder if your child drank Windex

✛

Time for your kid to say that in the
movie, the moon shoots a laser

✛

Time for you to ask: "Okay wait, is the bear named
Chewbacca, and his gun is a bowcaster, and the
'white people' are stormtroopers, and 'Santa Claus'
is actually Obi-Wan Kenobi, and the restaurant is the
Mos Eisley Cantina, and the moon that shoots the
laser is actually the Death Star, and the movie you're
describing is *Star Wars*, even though you mentioned
mostly auxiliary characters and minor plot points?"

✛

Time for your kid to say "Yes, and why is
your eye popping out of its socket?"

And finally, the Pythagorean Theorem of Parenting...

HOW LONG YOUR KIDS WILL
PLAY WITH A BLOW-UP TOY

Minutes you spent blowing it up with your mouth

1,000

THE ASSISTANT MANAGER

The most important skill a leader can have is the ability to delegate, which goes for parents too. You'll never have time for yourself if you're constantly swamped with the day-to-day minutiae of raising your kids, which is why you're going to unload it on a lackey.

In the world of business there is a position called the Assistant Manager. This person oversees a few mildly important duties, but they serve one critical purpose to the actual manager: They're a fall guy. A scapegoat. A punching bag. While the boss is relaxing in their cushy stockroom office with fluorescent lights and a fax machine precariously balanced on a pallet of Gatorade, the Assistant Manager is out on the floor mopping up spills, fielding customer complaints, and being called a prick by the entire staff. And what does the Assistant Manager happily take in return for doing this horrible job? An extra fifty cents an hour and a big set of keys.

Not everyone *wants* to be the Assistant Manager of course, which is why this title is usually given to a very specific type of person: power-hungry yet inept individuals with delusions of grandeur. And you know who else that describes? Literally every six-year-old.

Yes, you can quickly take a ton of unwanted parenting off your plate by "promoting" your oldest child to be the family's Assistant Manager. Make a huge deal out of it; maybe even give them a crown and a little sash. Their massive ego will actually make them *excited* to do your dirty work, and once they're intoxicated by this new perception of power, you can hit them with the harsh realities of their new job responsibilities.

FAMILY ASSISTANT MANAGER DAILY TASKS

○ Change and dispose of all dirty diapers produced by younger sibling

○ Kiss any owies, ouchies, scrapes, or boo-boos (while pretending this has medically sound health benefits)

○ Cook three balanced meals a day, even though the only thing younger sibling will eat is a hard-boiled egg and a handful of salami

○ Sit there and listen as younger sibling lists every shark they know (which is all of them)

○ Tantrum mediation

○ Broccoli negotiation

○ Cootie inoculation

○ Trim younger sibling's creepy little fingernails / possum claws

○ Find the answer to the question "Why is the baby sticky?"

○ And tattling, in exchange for immunity (snitches don't do dishes)

Once they've got their regular duties down, you can then lay out some long-term projects you'd like your Assistant Manager to tackle. If they don't want to change their younger sibling's diapers anymore, they should probably start potty training them. You showed *them* how to use the toilet, so now *they're* going to show the little one. And you already taught *one* kid to read—can you imagine starting over from scratch on that shit? But if you pass it off to the Assistant Manager, you'll amortize your ABC's efforts over two kids. That's just good business!

Inevitably your Assistant Manager will start to complain about how they're not really getting much benefit out of this arrangement, and it seems like they are doing all the work while you are drinking sangria. But say you've got them locked into an airtight contract, and if they'd like to formally address the issue they can bring it up during their yearly performance review. A 2 percent raise in allowance may be considered, and if they're not happy with that maybe their agent should have read the fine print.

On top of the time this will save you, the best part is the validation you'll get when your older child starts to make comments about how difficult it is to raise kids. Things like "It's so frustrating when Connor doesn't pick up his toys!" and "I spent so long making Connor that bologna sandwich. Why did he shove it in the mailbox?" It's like that moment at the end of *Undercover Boss* when the dickhead CEO tells his employees "I didn't realize how hard working in a warehouse is. I thought you guys *liked* peeing in Pepsi bottles and not having dental insurance!"

The one warning I will give is that you must keep a very close watch on the child you place in this role depending on their genetic predisposition to megalomania. One of the bigger mistakes my wife and I have made was when we told our daughter she was "like the third parent in our family" now that she had a baby brother. While we hoped this would inspire her to nurture and care for her infant sibling, it instead led to her making a power grab in a sort of kindergarten coup. She inserted herself into all high-level parenting decisions and even began forcing her brother to fetch her food and clean up after her. Essentially our Assistant Manager hired an *assistant* Assistant Manager, and we've spent the last several years trying to rebalance the hierarchy in our family like a low-stakes season of *Succession*. So before you bestow this kind of power on a child, just make sure it won't turn them into a Kid Jong-Un.

It's easy to feel like you're not a good parent unless you're completely overwhelmed, but don't be a martyr. You're not getting paid to do this, the job comes with no acclaim, so take advantage of the one remaining fringe benefit of being a boss: the right to dump work on your underlings and take all the credit.

WHEN TO BONE

The cruel irony of parenting is that the beautiful, ancient act that brings your children into this world (scientifically referred to as "raw dawging") then removes itself from your life entirely. This is because once you have kids, it's almost impossible to find time to squeeze it in. (I didn't mean that to be a sex pun, but I see now that it is. Please feel free to high-five this book.)

Your every waking moment is spent caring for the kids, so by the end of the day the only thing you have the time and energy to do is doze off while watching celebrities end their careers on *The Masked Singer*. If you're ever going to bring coitus back into your life, you'll need to carve out Grind Time where you'd least expect it. That's why I've created this list of time-conscious sex strategies that will give you and your partner a chance to smash, while ensuring your kids are completely unaware of the depraved acts you two are doing in the shadows.

SEE NO EVIL

My wife and I invented this one during a moment of desperate horniness when our first kid was just eight weeks old. Our daughter had fallen asleep in her baby seat, but like all new parents, we were terrified that if we walked more than ten feet away from our child she would instantly stop breathing. We obviously also didn't want her to wake up and see us flopping around on top of each other, so we just turned the baby seat to face the wall and had the most silent, no-frills sex in the history of man. Was the brief pleasure and personal connection outweighed by the immediate shame we felt? We're going to call it a tie, which for new parents is technically a win! (Also, if my daughter is reading this as an adult many years from now, I apologize for that imagery.)

CHARLES DICKIN' DOWN

Most people would not consider their local library a romantic destination, but remember: Horny is in the eye of the beholder. With a little creativity, any city-funded book depository can be a titillating site for a tryst. And why should this erotic locale only be enjoyed by your community's most public of masturbators? Most libraries have a weekly story-time event where the librarian reads kids whimsical tales about binge-eating caterpillars and sleepy neurotics who say goodnight to the moon. Take your child to one of these, and once the books start, loudly proclaim to the parent next to you, "AH CHRIST, I GOTTA TAKE A LEAK!" (You can say whatever you want to the person, but this particular phrase will result in no follow-up questions.) Ask them to keep an eye on your kid until you get back, then meet your partner in the least populated aisle in the library. My recommendations for this would be Advanced Geology, Albanian Fairy Tales, or Books by Ted Cruz. Hook up as quickly and, because this is a library, as *quietly*

as possible, then rejoin your child just in time to hear a story about Curious George, the monkey who seems like more trouble than he's worth.

BUBBLE BUMPIN'

Kids are unpredictable creatures, but the one behavior you can always rely on is that if they see Bubble Wrap, they will compulsively pop it, and not *stop* popping it until every little plastic pimple is burst. Here, you will use this unassailable law of science to the benefit of your quivering gonads. You can purchase a 175-foot roll of Bubble Wrap for a mere $25.99 on Amazon. As soon as the package arrives, use the overflowing sex hormones sloshing through your veins to tear it open like a Kodiak bear. Roll the Bubble Wrap out all over your house, and once your kids spot it, say, "Guys, whatever you do, do *not* pop this Bubble Wrap." This may feel counterintuitive, but the fact that you've politely asked them not to do this will make the act truly irresistible. At this point you and your betrothed can go up to your bedroom and wait for your moment to strike. At first you might think it'll never come, and that this could be the first time your children have ever actually followed your instructions. But like with a bag of microwave popcorn, you'll start to hear some sporadic pops, followed by a full-on barrage. You and your partner now have at least ten minutes to engage in rushed, almost-enjoyable boinking, the sounds of which will be completely drowned out by all the snaps, crackles, and pops emanating from the den.

THE HAMPTON HUMP

Getting a night away at a hotel is a common way for couples to rekindle some intimacy, but at this point the idea of both you and your partner leaving the kids for eighteen straight hours is a laughable nonstarter. You *can* go to a hotel for a *single* hour, however, using a move pioneered by our world's most ambitious sex workers. Book a room that's a short drive from your home, then get a babysitter to come watch the kids because you guys "have an important errand to run." Feel free to flex your creative muscles here. Maybe you have to "sign some tax documents," or perhaps you "have unfinished business with international drug kingpin Nacho de la Fuente." The details are up to you. Next, go to the hotel and check in. It will seem odd that you have no luggage, but tell the front desk clerk you're two acrobats fleeing the oppressive government of your home country . . . or perhaps you're at the hotel because you have unfinished business with international drug kingpin Nacho de la Fuente. Again, the details are up to you. At this point you and your betrothed are free to go up to the room, do your business, then shower off using tiny soaps wrapped in paper. And even though you are legally entitled to stay in this "suite" with a view of a commercial air-conditioning unit until 10 a.m. the following morning, you will now head home and relieve your babysitter, who will undoubtedly comment on how she's never seen you both smile at the same time.

"WE FORGOT THE ZITI!"

Get your family invited over to a friend's house for dinner, then spend the two weeks leading up to the meal bragging about how good your baked ziti recipe is. Tell your friends it's the same recipe your great-great-great-grandmother used to make back in Sicily that was once served to Pope Leo XII and made him weep with joy. Really lay it on thick, until your friends are like, "Jesus, this must be some great ziti." Then on the night of the dinner, show up to their house, unload your kids, and suddenly shout in unison with your spouse, "*Gasp!* We forgot the ziti!" Say the two of you are going to run home and grab it if your friend wouldn't mind watching the kids. (You both need to go, as one person couldn't possibly carry the amount of ziti you guys made.) You and your partner then speed home, make brisk love in the foyer, and drive back to dinner. When you reenter their house empty-handed and your friend asks where the ziti is, just say, "We have no idea what you're talking about."

It's common for us to place all our children's needs above our own, but remember that regularly connecting with your partner on a physical level is important to your relationship and should take some priority. So go ahead, you crazy lovebirds, light firecrackers off in the backyard to distract your kids while you do hand stuff in the toolshed. It's called *romance!*

UN-BLESS THIS MESS

According to research, the average child sneezes around four times a day. And after each of those sneezes we feel compelled to say the words "bless you," which takes around two seconds. That means per kid, we spend forty-eight minutes a year saying this phrase. And why? Because it's polite? Can you explain *why* it's polite? No, you cannot. Nobody can.

It's believed the reason we say "bless you" is because five hundred years ago people thought sneezing caused your soul to leave your body, and that saying "bless you" would momentarily protect you from Satan. You're wasting forty-eight minutes a year on *that*.

And when you expand this out to a family of four, you're suddenly pissing away over three hours a year trying to keep the Devil out of your nose. That's the entire runtime of Christopher Nolan's *Oppenheimer*! And God help you if you say "God" before "bless you." That's an additional twenty-four annual minutes down the tubes. In fact, let's not drag God into this at all. He's dealing with the whales and tornados and shit.

Just stop saying "bless you." That's all. Chapter over.

FIVE-SECOND STORIES

I love reading books to my kids at night. It's a great time to connect and gets them interested in literature from an early age. But when it comes to preserving your personal time as a parent, this is a risky part of the evening. That's because a "book" can mean a lot of different things to a kid. Sometimes it's an eight-pager you'll buzz right through; other times it's that thick collection of unnerving German nursery rhymes they got at a yard sale. And then there are the most insidious books of all, the "Five-Minute Stories."

This is a kids genre that has gotten very popular in recent years, but it is obviously not marketed toward children, because kids wish all stories lasted *infinite* minutes. No, the title "Five-Minute Stories" is aimed directly at exhausted parents. When you see that book coming off the shelf, it's a signal flare that says, "Only three-hundred more seconds until you can do what *you* want, which is eat an entire bag of Funyuns in elastic pants."

But as someone who has read many Five-Minute Stories at the end of a day that tested both my physical and emotional limits, I can tell you that five minutes is *way* too long. When you've slogged through twelve straight hours tending to your child's every whim, five more minutes feels like a prison sentence. So as a public service to parents everywhere, I've written a series of Five-*Second* Stories. These have all the whimsy of traditional children's books, but they'll get you through book time sixty times faster. So gather your kids and (very briefly) snuggle in.

THE HAPPY LITTLE TRUCK

The Happy Little Truck drove down the road.

Where was he going? Nobody knows!

First he turned right, then he turned left,

Then he was stolen, a case of grand theft.

(The police never found the guys.
Very common in cases like this.)

THE BUFFER-LO

*This is the story of Benny the brave little buffalo who
set out on a journey to find his herd, and . . . oh.
It looks like he's buffering.*

*Just give it a second . . .
the Wi-Fi has been weird today.*

*. . . Okay, we'll have to circle back on this.
I'll call Spectrum to come out and fix the router, but
it's going to be at least three to five business days.
Good night!*

SPANKY THE MATH SQUIRREL

This is Spanky the Math Squirrel!
Can you guess which number Spanky is thinking of?

You're right.

THE STORY THAT'S HAPPENING REALLY FAR AWAY

This is the tale of . . . what are those? Bugs?
Or, like . . . ninjas? Oh no, wait, maybe they're
dinosaurs or elephants or something. Actually,
now that I'm squinting, it kinda looks like
William H. Macy pushing a wheelbarrow. I can't
see a goddamn thing without my readers. Anyway,
whoever they are, they probably did something cool
or learned a lesson. Next story.

PUSH HERE!

Whoops. That was the End Story button.

Don't just be pushing random buttons, dude.

AMNESIA BADESIA!

This is Amnesia Badesia, the housekeeper
with short-term memory loss!
What's on your to-do list today, Amnesia?

Yikes.

THE DAY WHEN NOTHING HAPPENED

Most stories are about the day an ant climbed a mountain, or the day a dragon learned to hug, or or the day a bunny got the courage to drive a tractor, or the day a gecko discovered it's not so bad to lose your tail, or the day a plumber dug a giant hole and found out the Earth is made of marshmallows, or the day a puppy wearing a suit got elected president of the United States. But this story is about the day nothing *happened. It was honestly pretty chill, and everybody liked it.*

CINDERELLA
(BULLET POINT VERSION)

- Cinderella (orphan) lives with stepmother (evil) and has to do chores (boring)

- Loser prince with no game throws big party to find a wife (sad)

- Cinderella and prince dance one time and fall in love (clingy!)

- Cinderella loses shoe

- Prince says he'll marry whoever fits in shoe

- Prince finds Cinderella. They get married and live happily ever after, which is statistically unlikely considering she's a teen bride and they've only met once. But life expectancy in the 1700s was only like thirty-five, so who knows?

CAPTAIN LASER VERSUS THE SPACE PIRATES FROM PLANET Q!

Bang! Zoom!
Captain Laser pointed
his space rifle directly at the
approaching army of flying,
carnivorous super . . .

(NOTE FOR PARENTS ONLY: Let out a convincing gasp and exclaim, "Oh no! Someone spilled water on this page! It's completely illegible!")

Pirat... fro... the d... ded ... net ... These ... ates ar... now... or a num... er ... notab... char... erist... a, includi... their ... nchar... for cann... alis... and s... zzy o... its. C... ptain La... (who's ... irth n... ne was a... al... Claren... T. L... r IV, ... t he cha... ed wh... he jo... ed the ... ac... ader... so h... wou... t be cal... a "ne... baby... ro Clar... e ... aser l... rea... d his ... and, set ... sight... on s... ce Pir... s, ... d let o... h's ... natu... and high... merc... ndisal... cat... nt ... e "It's ... er ... !" A... hat hero... (and, a... in, hi... ly. mer... n... able) ... ttle ... rang ... ut o... er t... cosmo... the ... ur Pir... s w... re va... zed ... Cap... n La... er... ighty ... st. A... ok i... ne h... cl... bed b... k int... is ro... et po... took a... mirr... rook ... deep ... reath, a... smiled

"That was a cool mission," said Captain Laser.

The End. Go to bed.

Are the kids asleep? No? Who cares. You have fulfilled your legal obligation to read a story in record time, and are now free to waste the hour you just saved by researching your various physical ailments on WebMD. Enjoy, you've earned it.

THE PERFECT PARENTING SCHEDULE

One of the most popular productivity tools around is called "time blocking." It was created back in the Bronze Age and even used by confirmed pervert Benjamin Franklin (google it!). The idea is that you break your forthcoming day into distinct blocks of time, then plan out what you're going to do in each of those periods to maximize efficiency. Using this ancient wisdom, I have plotted out what I believe to be the Perfect Parenting Schedule. This is an entire day of parental life distilled into productive, actionable chunks of time that will help you accomplish everything your children throw at you, while ensuring you also get a little time for yourself. Let's begin!

5:00 A.M.: Wake up. Say "Ugh, fuck."

5:15 A.M.: Pray to God kids sleep in today.

5:30 A.M.: Hear kids fighting. Remember God is dead.

5:45 A.M.: Dump coffee down your throat while unreasonable breakfast orders are shouted at you.

6:00 A.M.: Try to figure out what it means to cook "an omelet but with NO EGGS!"

6:15 A.M.: Serve breakfast. Be called "fat" in a hurtful yet accurate comment from your toddler.

6:30 A.M.: Try to make your own breakfast—realize the kids have eaten all the yogurt, bread, fruit, and cereal.

6:45 A.M.: Convince yourself that there must be some country where they eat "breakfast soup."

7:00 A.M.: Scrub chowder out of your bathrobe.

7:15 A.M.: Look for kid's shoe.

7:30 A.M.: Continue looking for shoe.

7:45 A.M.: Find shoe in microwave, the place where all shoes go.

8:00 A.M.: See your kid get unbelievably excited at the sight of a garbage truck. Relive every interaction you've ever had with him and question if he actually loves you.

8:15 A.M.: Attempt to poop. Abort mission when you hear one kid tell the other one to "Put down the knife!"

8:30 A.M.: Stare at yourself in the mirror for a little too long remembering that you have a master's degree.

8:45 A.M.: Put in load of laundry because one kid is wearing a bathing suit as underwear.

9:00 A.M.: Attempt to poop again. Get thwarted by a teary-eyed child asking, "If the dinosaurs died, am *I* going to die?"

9:15 A.M.: Explain the dinosaurs only died because a giant meteor smashed into the planet and killed them all.

9:30 A.M.: Assure your kid a meteor could never smash into the planet today (even though you both know that's a lie).

9:45 A.M.: Switch laundry to dryer. Realize one of your child's pockets was filled with loose glitter. Whisper the worst curse word you can think of into a nearby jar.

10:00 A.M.: Check the clock, thinking it must be afternoon by now. Let despair permeate your every atom.

10:15 A.M.: Your kids ask for juice and you say no because it's too sugary. Reflect on the unfairness of how when you were a kid juice was a health food, but now that you could be giving it to *your* kids it's treated like drinkable fentanyl.

10:30 A.M.: Take laundry out of the dryer. Place on the counter where it will sit unfolded until Labor Day.

10:45 A.M.: Pretend to be excited about a leaf your kid found.

11:00 A.M.: Get asked to gather every chair, pillow, sheet, and towel in the house so your kids can build a fort.

11:15 A.M.: Get strong-armed into building the fort yourself.

11:30 A.M.: Get criticized for your fort-building skills.

11:45 A.M.: Mention that before you were a parent, you were actually an architect, which is a person who designs buildings in the real world. Watch your kids walk away before you even finish that sentence.

12:00 P.M.: Make first kid lunch, which is not appreciated.

12:15 P.M.: Make second kid lunch, which is neither appreciated nor eaten.

12:30 P.M.: Kid sneezes directly up your nose. Google "Purell in nostrils?"

12:45 P.M.: Children ask to go to the park. Begin applying sunscreen to children.

1:00 P.M.: Continue applying sunscreen to children.

1:15 P.M.: Continue applying sunscreen to children.

1:30 P.M.: Continue applying sunscreen to children.

1:45 P.M.: Continue applying sunscreen to children.

2:00 P.M.: Continue applying sunscreen to children.

2:15 P.M.: Continue applying sunscreen to children.

2:30 P.M.: Carry both kids to the park because they are "too tired."

2:45 P.M.: Get to the park. Watch kids who are "too tired" run faster than you have ever run in your entire life.

3:00 P.M.: Leave park because one kid sat in a puddle and the other is scared of a bush.

3:15 P.M.: Get home. Stand by helplessly as kids empty the sand from their socks into your vegetable crisper.

3:30 P.M.: Be asked to set up Hasbro's Mouse Trap, which is less of a game and more of a jury summons.

3:45 P.M.: Play Mouse Trap alone because the kids got bored before setup was complete. Remember a time in your life when you had interests and hobbies.

4:00 P.M.: Break up a fight about a pencil.

4:15 P.M.: Break up a fight about Corn Nuts.

4:30 P.M.: Break up a fight about dolphins.

4:45 P.M.: Break up a fight about whether infinity is bigger than the number 91.

5:00 P.M.: Begin prepping dinner.

5:15 P.M.: Cook dinner.

5:30 P.M.: Pretend your recipe requires a red wine reduction, then suck down the remaining 95 percent of the bottle yourself so it "doesn't go bad."

5:45 P.M.: Serve the sausage dish you've made.

6:00 P.M.: Be told "Sausage is gross," then get asked for a hot dog.

6:15 P.M.: Explain that hot dogs *are* sausages. Lose argument. Make hot dog.

6:30 P.M.: Sit down to eat your sausage dish.

6:45 P.M.: Watch with melancholy as your children sit on your lap and eat said sausage dish right off your plate while exclaiming, "Wow, this is *good*!"

7:00 P.M.: Consume your new dinner, which is your child's half-eaten hot dog and a single grape.

7:15 P.M.: Say "Okay, guys, time to clean up." Repeat forty times, somehow being ignored more on each subsequent declaration.

7:30 P.M.: Wonder, "Do my kids not respect me, or can they not hear me because I've died and become a ghost?"

7:45 P.M.: Be called "fat" for the second time today, confirming you *are* still alive and *still* not respected.

8:00 P.M.: Bathe your children while they yell at you.

8:15 P.M.: Brush your children's teeth while they yell at you.

8:30 P.M.: Put on your children's jammies while they yell at you.

8:45 P.M.: Give hugs and read stories and do dances and sing songs to the children who have just been screaming at you for forty-five minutes.

9:00 P.M.: Finally get kids down, two hours later than intended.

9:15 P.M.: Oh hey look both kids are already out of bed and just fuckin' walking around.

9:30 P.M.: Field a number of half-baked pitches from your children as to why they can't fall asleep, including "My eyebrow hurts" and "I'm worried it will rain next week."

9:45 P.M.: Put kids back in bed. Research if locking kids in their room is "legal" or "okay."

10:00 P.M.: Kids are asleep. Finally poop.

10:15 P.M.: Try to watch that documentary everyone says is so great. Fall asleep in chair before the Netflix logo is even done.

10:30 P.M.: Continue sleeping with your neck contorted so aggressively that you will never fully recover from this nap.

10:45 P.M.: Startle yourself awake when you remember your kid's lucky sweater isn't washed and if it's not clean in the morning, *you* are gonna be unlucky.

11:00 P.M.: Eat ten thousand calories in old Halloween candy you find hidden behind the detergent. It has that gross chalky stuff chocolate gets on it when it's a year old, but you eat it anyway in an attempt to avoid being alone with your feelings.

11:15 P.M.: One of the kids is up again saying he saw a vampire in his room biting a baby kitten. And of course you don't believe in vampires, but the "biting a baby kitten" thing was so oddly specific you're no longer 100 percent skeptical of the supernatural.

11:30 P.M.: Snuggle with kid to get them back to sleep (and grab a clove of garlic just in case of the vampire thing).

11:45 P.M.: Bat cleanup on that Halloween candy. You don't even *enjoy* Almond Joys, but again, the feelings.

CONGRATULATIONS! YOU MADE IT TO MIDNIGHT!

You now have five uninterrupted hours to work on yourself, pursue your passions, practice self-care, catch up on your to-do list, and have a little *fun*! You'll get it all in, just stick to the schedule!

12:00 A.M.: Learn French.

12:15 A.M.: Do taxes.

12:30 A.M.: Meal prep for the month.

12:45 A.M.: Answer your three hundred unread emails.

1:00 A.M.: Do ten thousand sit-ups.

1:15 A.M.: Empty gutters.

1:30 A.M.: Vacuum (quietly!).

1:45 A.M.: Watch the trailer for your favorite movie (no time for full film).

2:00 A.M.: Come up with idea for a book.

2:15 A.M.: Pitch book (to UK publishers, only ones that are awake at this hour).

2:30 A.M.: Sell book.

2:45 A.M.: Write book.

3:00 A.M.: Publish book. Become rich, world-famous author.

3:15 A.M.: Clean dishwasher filter.

3:30 A.M.: Become smart by reading one news article about "important issues."

3:45 A.M.: Finally figure out which haircut is right for your face.

4:00 A.M.: Learn to play the oboe.

4:15 A.M.: Take up woodworking.

4:30 A.M.: Build a kayak, row it across a lake.

4:45 A.M.: Sleep.

5:00 A.M.: Wake up. Say "Ugh, fuck."

It's that simple. Just repeat this every day for the next eighteen to twenty-five years and you really can have it all!

MILLION-DOLLAR IDEAS: TIME-SAVER EDITION

Throughout this book I will be giving away ideas for inventions that are worth millions (probably even *billions*) of dollars to parents. I don't personally know how to design things or build things or patent things, so I am providing these concepts free of charge in the hope that you more industrious parents will pick up the torch, manufacture these, and give me one at a steep discount. As we close out this section on saving time, my first set of inventions are designed to do exactly that.

THE CRUST GUILLOTINE

Kids hate crust. Even though it provides critical infrastructure to their sandwiches *and* is bread-flavored, they simply cannot fathom eating it. So parents can spend upward of fifty hours a week engaging in crust management and removal, but the Crust Guillotine will cut that time down by 300 percent! And while this may just look like four butcher knives tied together, that's only because that's exactly what it is. One forceful thrust down with

this on a grilled cheese will leave any sandwich crustless in no time, freeing you up to do more important things like drive yourself to the emergency room to reattach your fingers.

PRE-BUILT LEGOS

There is an age range (three to five) when kids *think* they want to build LEGOs but still have the attention span of a hummingbird on methamphetamines. They'll beg you to open up a set and dump out all the pieces, only to abandon you while you sit alone, snapping millions of tiny bricks together using an instruction booklet longer than the New Testament. But with Pre-Built LEGOs, everything is already assembled for you. That way, you and your child can skip ahead to the end of every LEGO build: that disappointing moment when you say, "Oh wow look, it's a horse."

CINNAMON TOOTH CRUNCH

In those final high-pressure moments before they need to leave for school, your kids often run out the clock on all feeding and hygiene routines in an attempt to avoid brushing their teeth for the tenth time that week. So tomorrow morning you'll be serving them a heaping bowl of Cinnamon Tooth Crunch! These toothpaste-infused wheat squares are part of a balanced breakfast *and* chock-full of tasty monofluorophosphates, guaranteed to fill their bellies and battle the widow-maker known as gingivitis. While four out of five dentists definitely *do not* recommend feeding your children food secretly laced with Aquafresh, that fifth dentist is a crazy sonofabitch and he *loves* it.

VEL-CLOTHES

Kids are constantly losing everything they own, and it's common to spend your whole day searching for their "necessary" supplies, like a torn *Doc McStuffins* bookmark or that stick of beef jerky they've been slowly eating since Wednesday. That's why your child needs Vel-Clothes (the Velcro Clothes). This is a bodysuit covered in heavy-duty Velcro strong enough to adhere items both large and small directly to your kid's body. Do they keep forgetting to bring their water bottle to school? Stick it to their head. Can they never find their shoes? Tuck a back-up pair of Keds in each armpit. While there *is* a high probability your child will brush up against a neighborhood cat that will get permanently stuck to their leg, that's okay. It can eat the beef jerky.

THE "HEY LOOK!" HOLOGRAM

For half a century, hologram technology has only been available to Starfleet officers and Tupac Shakur. But now we're going to use it to bring parenting into the twenty-fifth century. The "Hey Look!" Hologram is an artificially intelligent cybernetic replica of your own sad body, which is activated the three to four hundred times a day your child yells the wake phrase "Hey look!" Your digital doppelgänger will suddenly materialize and gaze intently as your child does the same (subpar) dance move for an hour, giving you ample time to watch videos of people making Doritos pasta on TikTok.

OKAY, SO NOW YOU'VE GOT FREE TIME . . .

YOU DID IT. You've mastered time. You are Marty McFly. You are Loki. You are Bill and/or Ted. You're reading books, watching prestige dramas on HBO, and having sex that is more than semiannual. You finally have room in your schedule for all the activities you've been longing to do since that fateful day you procreated. The thing you regrettably *don't* have right now is cash.

When you weren't looking, you got sucked into the Ponzi scheme known as "parenting," and all your new discretionary time won't amount to much if you can't bankroll the fabulous new lifestyle that's finally within your reach. But don't worry, because the next step of our voyage is going to refill your coffers (whatever the fuck those are). Now that you've got time, it's time to get you paid. . . .

PART II

Your Money

Experts say it takes over $300,000 to raise a child today. That's about $18,000 a year for eighteen years in a row. Then those children might go to college, where you can spend an additional $200,000 for them to learn about "Communications" and forget it all when they butt-chug vodka at a Frisbee tournament. And what do you get for this half-million-dollar investment? An adult who doesn't call you on your birthday and fills your basement with DJ equipment.

Those are just the base costs too. There are many hidden fees kids accumulate in the background, similar to a gym membership or the Rosé of the Month club you *allegedly* joined during that bachelorette party in Napa. You also need to account for the expensive stuff they break, the perfectly good food they waste, and the times you'll have to hire a plumber to remove a decapitated Bratz doll from your garbage disposal (an idea you're convinced your child got from a Saw movie that night they slept over at the weird kid's house).

From a dollars and cents perspective, kids are a horrible business decision with little hope of return on investment—except for the gamble they might let you live in their garage one day when you can no longer butter your own toast. For the amount of money it takes to raise a child, you could buy an income property, or retire early, or hire Kim Kardashian to crash her private plane into Jeff Bezos's small penis super-boat.

We love having kids, though. The ways they enrich our lives mostly make up for the ways they de-rich our bank accounts. But that doesn't mean we shouldn't try to get this whole thing done on the cheap. We're now going to increase your cash flow by scrutinizing your parenting budget line by line. In this section I will teach you how to save on everything from soccer fees to Christmas trees, turn your gross home into gross income, and give your kid a first-class existence by defrauding America's most detestable billionaires. Consider the next pillar of this book a promo code wrapped in a Memorial Day mattress sale atop a fresh bed of Bed Bath & Beyond coupons.

You are the CEO of your family, and like all successful CEOs you need to slash overhead, squeeze the little guy, and funnel all those profits to the shareholders (which hey, guess what, are also you). So buckle up, baby. We're gettin' frugal.

DIY OB-GYN

Bringing a child into this world can cost around $3,000 if you have insurance and a massive $20K without it. Call me old-fashioned, but I think it should be much cheaper to pull something out than put something in. Installing a new kitchen? Eighty grand. Demolishing one? Give fifty bucks to a drunk guy with a hammer.

But the birth of your kid doesn't have to be expensive. Think about it, who charges you all that money? *The hospital.* So that's exactly who we're going to remove from the equation. Granted, giving birth at a hospital is much, much, *much* safer than the alternatives (i.e., the method your sister found on Reddit where you give birth in a plastic pool like you're running a salmon hatchery). But if you're looking to start your parenting career in the black, here are a few budget-conscious delivery options.

LOITER IN A MEDICAL SCHOOL DINING HALL

Find the medical school that's closest to your home, then spend the week you're due wandering around the student food court making friendly eye contact with all the nerds. When you finally do go into labor, you won't be near any "professional" "doctors," but this is like when you go to a beauty school to get a discount haircut: These kids will try their darndest and get *pretty close* to the real thing. As you prop your feet up on two stacks of lunch trays, let all three hundred nearby pupils gather around your dilated cervix as they nervously mutter, "Oh my God oh my God oh my

God"—then nominate someone to catch the baby by pointing at the student with the biggest hands and bellowing "YOU!" Theoretically the students' amateur understanding of the birthing process will be outweighed by the sheer number of them, and they'll deliver your baby faster than that Quiznos you're flashing can deliver a Spicy Monterey sub. You may then dab your new bundle of joy off with brown paper napkins and be on your way.

ESTIMATED COST: Free.

SIDE BENEFITS: You'll be surrounded by lots of good baby name inspiration, like "Jersey Mike" and "Sbarro."

POTENTIAL DOWNSIDE: Salad bar episiotomy.

FENDER REVEAL PARTY

On the day you're due, wait in your car outside a medical center parking lot. Once your contractions are five minutes apart, strap on a helmet and gently (*gently!!!*) rear-end the nicest car you see leaving the garage. Chances are the driver of that vehicle will be a doctor (and depending on the trim level of their convertible, probably one of the good ones). Insist that there's just no time to go inside the hospital and they're going to have to deliver your baby right there on the center divider. Then pop a squat, focus up, and use the horrified honks of passing motorists as motivation to push. When the doctor asks why you're wearing a helmet, say you are famed NFL quarterback Russell Wilson.

ESTIMATED COST: Repair of a BMW bumper (approximately $1,200).

SIDE BENEFITS: You're married to Ciara!

POTENTIAL DOWNSIDE: You accidentally rear-end a podiatrist, who only pulls out the baby's feet then leaves.

THE VIETNAMESE TAXI METHOD

We've all heard of the occasional baby being born in a taxi, but there's a cab company in Vietnam that practically specializes in it. They're called the Mai Linh Group, and they proudly hold the title for "Delivering the Maximum Number of Newborn Babies in Taxi Cars" from the *Asia Book of Records*. Between the years of 2008 and 2020 their drivers helped deliver a whopping *191 babies* during trips. They are like Uber for your uterus. You thought that driver who made a U-turn to pick you up was helpful? My dudes are cauterizing C-section incisions with a 12-volt cigarette lighter. When your due date approaches, just book a trip to Vietnam, stand on a busy street corner, and as soon as you see the baby's head pop out, flag down one of the Mai Linh Group's bright green cabs. I don't care how much you love your doctor, you simply cannot beat the cost and convenience of having a nice young man named Quang delivering your baby in the backseat of his Camry, all in exchange for a fist bump and a five-star rating.

ESTIMATED COST: Flight to Ho Chi Minh City (approximately $1,300 USD). Two-kilometer ride in a cab (approximately 30,000 Vietnamese Dong).

SIDE BENEFITS: Complimentary water and mints.

POTENTIAL DOWNSIDE: Quang doing his best to teach you Lamaze through Google Translate.

FORCE A CASUAL ACQUAINTANCE TO
BECOME A GYNECOLOGIST

This is a long game, but the savings potential is massive. During your senior year of high school, long before you're married or even thinking about having a child, identify your most suggestible friend—the type of guy who would easily join a multilevel marketing scheme and thinks David Copperfield is actually magic. This individual doesn't even need to be your friend, could just be the aw-shucks guy you sit next to in biology. Whoever it is, really build him up. Start small with compliments like "Wow, Greg, you're *so* smart" and "Greg, has anyone ever told you your hands are soft while also being both dexterous and muscular?" Then gradually become a bit more direct with your flattery, saying things like "Greg, you are *great* with kids" and "You know *every* part of the female reproductive system. You should do something with that!" At some point, or perhaps many points, Greg will think you are hitting on him, so make it abundantly clear you find him sexually repulsive. You're just encouraging your good friend Greg (whatever his last name is) to follow his passion, one that he himself has never expressed any real interest in. Keep up this relentlessly supportive ruse through all four of Greg's years in undergrad, his four years of medical school, and his four years of gynecological residency. You should be having your first child *right* around the time Greg receives his medical license, and what better way to repay a friend for twelve years of curiously aggressive encouragement than pulling a baby out of them for free?

ESTIMATED COST: Nothing (for you ... Greg will incur hundreds of thousands of dollars in student debt).

SIDE BENEFITS: It's fun to tell people what to do.

POTENTIAL DOWNSIDE: None (for you ... Greg's life has been squandered. But that's what he gets for being such a Greg).

ELLEN POMPEO

If you can't guilt a real doctor into delivering your child, the next best option is one of our nation's many TV doctors (who are just like real doctors but hotter). And no TV doctor has more fictional medical expertise than American treasure Ellen Pompeo. While pretending to be an M.D. is not even close to real hospital experience, she has portrayed Meredith Grey on *Grey's Anatomy* for over twenty years, so she must have picked up *something*, right? For this strategy, you're going to need to use your private eye skills to find out where Ellen Pompeo shops, eats, does Pilates, and pumps her gas—then start frequenting those places yourself. It's very important to not do anything illegal or creepy here, just keep "accidentally" running into Ellen Pompeo three times a day for the last two weeks of your pregnancy. That way when your water breaks in front of her at Costco, you two will already have a relationship and she'll jump into action maybe!

ESTIMATED COST: $300 for stalking gas; $500 for cool maternity detective outfits.

SIDE BENEFITS: *Costco Connection* magazine will likely do a photo spread with you, your baby, and Ellen Pompeo.

POTENTIAL DOWNSIDE: Hollywood is fake and actors aren't actually like the people they portray on TV (unlikely).

Much like new cars, kids start to depreciate the second they leave the lot/womb. So don't get conned into paying a hefty down payment and dealer fees. You know who also wasn't born in a hospital? Abraham Lincoln. And his face is printed on money! Money you'll get to keep in your pocket when Ellen Pompeo cuts your umbilical cord using a pair of Kirkland brand garden shears.

KLEPTO-CURRENCY

There are many unfair parts about being a parent. You can't eat at restaurants that don't serve curly fries. You have to drive around in a minivan with big sliding doors like you're flying a Coast Guard helicopter. But the most unjust aspect of this whole thing is that while your kids are a massive financial drain on you, there are times during their childhood when they themselves actually become quite rich (relatively speaking).

Children receive small injections of petty cash consistently throughout the year by way of birthdays, Valentine cards from Grandma, and digging nickels out of public gumball machines that are somehow still legal in a post-COVID world. Since kids have zero financial responsibilities, that money's pure profit, and over time they amass a nest egg of no-strings-attached discretionary funds that acts as a kindergarten super PAC. Your children are bleeding you dry *and* have more fun money than you, and we need to put a stop to this.

So I've concocted a way to both rein in your kids' spending and recoup the most ridiculous costs of parenting directly from the people who incur them. Is it moral? Not really. But neither are your children.

So from now on, whenever your kid "makes" money, you're going to hold on to it for "safekeeping." (They misplace everything, allowing you to spin this as a service provided out of the kindness of your heart.) But the catch is that now if they want to buy something stupid, they need you to approve the withdrawal. And if they *do* something stupid that costs *you* money, you now have the ability to garnish their wages like the IRS. You've essentially pulled off a hostile corporate merger and installed yourself as their chief financial officer, which gives you the leverage in a number of scenarios:

- Let's say you're at a restaurant and your child demands to order off the adult menu, but when their platter of pan-seared king salmon arrives they refuse to take a single bite. You are now entitled to quietly remove $28.32 from their piggy bank.

- Notice an $8 charge on your iTunes account because your son bought a game called *Boob Simulator*? You've just qualified for a handful of reimbursement quarters.

- Trip to the ER when your kid hits her brother in the face with a garden hose, immediately after you said the phrase "Be careful, you're about to hit your brother in the face with that garden hose"? Go ahead and repossess a significant portion of your insurance deductible.

On top of financial restitution, this system serves another important function: It keeps your kid below a certain salary cap to ensure they never obtain what investment experts call "Fuck You Mom and Dad Money." This is a level of child wealth (which does not have to be very much, by the way) where your kids can buy truly outlandish shit and there's not much you can do about it. I know because it happened to me.

I write for a late-night TV show, and during the height of the pandemic we had to get creative with how we filmed sketches. This was still in that "scrub your bananas with Clorox wipes while crying" period, so instead of bringing actors to our studio, we'd often cast our staff members and their kids, then record them from home in the name of health and safety. One day we were shooting a bit about kids doing Zoom school, so I told the crew they could use my daughter to play a one-line part they needed to fill. This offhand comment has caused me four years of strife (and counting).

That's because when people appear on a union television show, they get paid. And they also get something called "residual checks," which is when they receive additional money whenever their work is rerun. So all of a sudden, because my child said nine words on TV in the middle of the night, she had $700 cash. For an adult, that's about a week's worth of living expenses, but to a six-year-old that's like winning the Powerball. And from that day forward our daughter has lived like 50 Cent in a strip club.

She is now financially invincible. If we deny her request to get ice cream, she insists on paying for it. Not just for her, but for the whole family. "I'll get ya all thirty-one flavors, baby!" And like a little lobbyist, she's even begun using her money to influence others. We found out that at a playdate our daughter dared a couple of kids to jump into a cold pool, and when they hesitated, she peeled them off a couple of twenties to sweeten the deal. "Here . . . go dry off and buy yourself some Hatchimals."

Emboldened by her new ability to pay off her friends, our daughter came up with an even bigger scheme. She had been begging us for weeks to take her to Petco so she could buy a ceramic cat figurine they sell there, but we don't have any pets and weren't super into the idea of making an unnecessary trip to an iguana-fart warehouse. So to circumvent us, our daughter snuck some cash to school and gave it to her friend. A friend who then talked *her* mom into driving to Petco, for the sole purpose of buying this cat figurine for our daughter (a child she had never met). And it *worked*! By putting my kid on TV for three and a half seconds, I had inadvertently zapped her with a powerful form of Nepo Baby Radiation, and she was now smuggling money and goods across the playground like an elementary school El Chapo.

All this to say, it's okay to take money from your kids. In fact, you *must*. It may feel like stealing, but think about it this way: You created your kids from nothing; therefore you kinda own your kids—no different than how you would own a casserole you prepared from scratch. So by the transitive property, *you* own everything *they* own, and you can't really steal from yourself now can you? Plus kids probably shouldn't have money anyway, for the same reason you shouldn't give a gun to a monkey: Maybe it'll be fine, but that's also how the Planet of the Apes got started.

EXER-SIGHS

One of the first things the parenting process claims is your physique. Maybe you were never going to win a triathlon or join Leonardo DiCaprio's harem of yacht floozies, but you were doing all right. Then once you had kids your body quickly began to resemble a Ziploc bag of reheated chili, and unfortunately gym memberships and personal trainers cost a *lot* of money. Money you now have to spend on summer camps and Super Mario underpants.

While the hope of true fitness has been torn from our lives, the good news is it has been replaced by new and, most importantly, *free* real-world opportunities for exercise. As it says in the Bible: "When God closes a door, he opens a Planet Fitness." So let's kill two birds with one rock-hard ab.

REMOVING YOUR TODDLER FROM A BOUNCE HOUSE

DESCRIPTION: It's hour three of your child's classmate's birthday party (even though they coulda done this whole thing in seventeen minutes!). You've spent your afternoon in the park making excruciating small talk with a variety of bizarre parents, but the goodie bags have been distributed and you are legally free to go. All you have to do is collect your spawn and get the hell out of there, but unfortunately your kid snuck back into the bounce house when you weren't looking and is refusing to leave. Now you must physically remove them, and while this extraction process always has some collateral damage, you can't spell *collateral* with "lats," so let's work 'em!

MUSCLES WORKED: Deltoids, Biceps, Laterals, Your Patience.

MOTION: Start with your feet shoulder-width apart. Keep your core engaged as you hinge at the hip, extend your arm forward, and use your dominant hand to grasp your child's disgusting little foot. As your kid shrieks at ear-piercing volumes, pull their sweaty hoof toward you while bending at the elbow and wondering what kinds of happy hour cocktails your childless friends are drinking right now. You hate them. Deeply. But funnel that rage down to your tricep and continue to tug. It is at this point your child's sock will slip off and they'll scurry back into the bounce house like a ferret. Repeat reps until you pass out from frustration and the most annoying dad at the party offers to drive you to the hospital on his moped.

BABY GATE GODZILLA

DESCRIPTION: In an attempt to make your baby laugh, you pretended to be a giant monster climbing over their baby gate like Godzilla attacking a city. This was a huge mistake because it *did* make your baby laugh, which means you will be performing this debilitating physical task over and over until one of you falls asleep. Luckily this slightly amusing bit can give you all the fitness benefits of a rock climbing sesh from the discomfort of your own home.

MUSCLES WORKED: Quadriceps, Gluteals, Rotator Cuffs, Kaiju Posterior.

MOTION: First, grip the creaking frame of your kitchen door and hoist yourself up, placing an immense amount of faith in this deteriorating two-by-four and the contractor with tuberculosis who installed it in the 1930s. Now that you are suspended in the air like a tubby Tom Cruise, all the muscles in your legs and torso will begin to seize violently. This pain will be sharp and unceasing, but use it as motivation for the beast-like roar your baby demands you make with each and every repetition. With your Croc pointed outward, forcefully swing the deadweight of your leg over the gate as if you're an elderly cowboy mounting a horse. Even though every fiber of your body is pleading for you to stop this madness, you are currently spread-eagle over a Toddleroo Easy Close and there's no going back now. With one final thrust, vault your second leg over the gate, slumping to the floor with a disconcerting *thunk*. Much like the real Godzilla, you will now feel like a prehistoric lizard suffering from radiation poisoning, so take some hard-earned rest in the one second you have before your child yells "again!"

"I FORGOT THE STROLLER"

DESCRIPTION: You planned a day with the kids at a botanical garden—which, you know, is fine. No one's ever been *excited* to go to a botanical garden, but at least this will be better than sitting at home watching the kids burp on each other. Or, you *thought* it would be better, until you got to the gardens and realized you forgot to pack the stroller. The stroller is the backbone to any outing with children: It's a limousine, food truck, medical tent, and cargo barge all rolled into one, but because you neglected to bring it, *you* are now the stroller. That's okay though, because this is a great excuse to engage in an all-day HIIT-style full-body workout.

MUSCLES WORKED: ALL.

MOTION: To begin, bend your knees until your thighs

are parallel to the ground. Raise your arms out to the side just below shoulder level and allow yourself to be loaded up like a pack mule that's about to embark on a twelve-day trek through the Columbia River Gorge. Breathe deeply to relax your muscles. This will make it easier for your kids to fill every crack and crevice of your body with "important" items they brought from home, including dump trucks, glitter pens, and (even though you're at a garden, which is literally *made* of sticks) a stick. Once your kids climb aboard, straighten your legs into a standing position while emitting that deep guttural sound your grandpa used to make whenever he got out of a lawn chair. Now with your shoulders slouched forward so your head hangs in shame, walk nonstop for the next four to six hours while mosquitoes eat your cankles.

SNACK BITCH

DESCRIPTION: Your family's finally ready for the 800-mile road trip to visit your mother-in-law in Scottsbluff, Nebraska, and your spouse quickly agrees to drive the entire way. *That's nice!* you think, until the second the car rolls out of the driveway and the kids start ordering snacks from you like you're the waiter at a tapas restaurant. It is only then you realize you are the trip's designated "Snack Bitch." This is a title my wife coined to describe the thankless job of the parent riding shotgun on a long drive, which is basically a cross between a hotel concierge and a bus stop vending machine. You're about to spend an entire day slingin' Saltines, but it's not all bad, because this relentless core workout will have your trunk

ripped by the time you reach the Cornhusker State!
MUSCLES WORKED: Rectus Abdominis, Obliques,
Cheeto Fingers.

MOTION: Holding two arms full of snacks with flavors
like "Cheddar Blast" and "BLUE!" slowly exhale as you
rotate your torso toward the unreasonable occupants
of the seats behind you. Use rapid-fire tricep extensions
to present your children with various corn-syruped
foodstuffs, performing hundreds of reps as they reject
every single offering (even though these are really all
just the same cracker shaped like slightly different
Transformers). Once both you and your options have
been exhausted, sigh deeply as you twist back toward the
dashboard and pivot downward to forage through your
backpack for more acceptable refreshments, as if you
are a fucking 7-Eleven or something. You will work up
quite an appetite during this routine, but DO NOT EAT
from the kid snack stockpile. A single bite has enough
sodium to put you in the ICU.

POOL BITCH

DESCRIPTION: If you thought being Snack Bitch was
tiring, you've never been "Pool Bitch." This is the one
parent in the pool who the kids nominate to be a raft,
diving board, landing pad, submarine, referee, goggle
fixer, and baby lifeguard all at once. And not just for
your kids. Because you were dumb enough to dive in,
you now must provide these services for every slippery
little weirdo in this urinal-scented community pool.
There's an upside though, because while water aerobics

are usually reserved for sexy seniors, anyone can use the position of Pool Bitch to develop Poseidon-level strength and fishlike reflexes.

MUSCLES WORKED: Pectorals, Traps, Hamstrings, Dorsal Flab.

MOTION: Warm up by standing waist-deep in the water while every child in the pool quizzically examines your middle-aged body like you're the subject of a nature documentary. Be prepared for such questions as "Why do you have hair in there?" and "Did your nipples always look like that?" Press your heels into the pool floor, doing hip rotations as you identify which of these countless untamed children don't actually know how to swim, because you will be saving their lives every few seconds for the next several hours. Next, place one hand on your head at a ninety-degree angle to make a fin, because the kid with the bad haircut swimming in a *Fortnite* T-shirt just shouted, "Hey old guy, be a shark!" Continue this pose until you hear the next command phrase, which is "Hey old guy, catch me!" yelled by a child with what appears to be a violently contagious rash. Then play Marco Polo. Then do an underwater handstand. Then teach a kid the backstroke. Then stop a random infant from getting sucked into the pool filter . . . all while staring incredulously at these kids' very dry parents who are sitting in deck chairs watching Sydney Sweeney's Instagram stories.

PENIS PUNCH / TIT KICK

DESCRIPTION: This is less of an exercise and more of an endurance regimen, like doing an ice bath or appearing in a Jackass movie. Somewhere between one and one thousand times a day, parents are roundhouse kicked in the genitals by a 3T sneaker. This is extremely unpleasant, but if instead of trying to avoid it, you welcome the blunt gonad trauma with pride like a Roman gladiator, you will eventually become desensitized to all forms of pain both physical and spiritual. Bear down, embrace the agony, and soon, nothing will stop you.

MUSCLES WORKED: Penis and/or Tit.

MOTION: The best part about this is you don't have to move or even *choose* to do it. It is the only exercise that happens *to* you. Just go about your life, and when you least expect it (even though at this point, you definitely *should* expect it) you'll be booted so hard in the nards it'll make your entire life flash before your eyes. As the pain pulses out to every corner of your anatomy, tense up each muscle in your body until the throbbing dissipates (assuming it ever dissipates). Now stiffen your upper lip, ask for another, and become the steel-dicked/-titted Terminator you were always meant to be—just as the prophecy foretold.

Are you sexy now? No, definitely not. In fact, you better not be. Don't let those online #FitParents shame you. If you're raising your kids well, you can't also have a body like the statue of David. I say, aim for the body of *Larry* David: scrappy, spry, unpredictable, bald. And you don't get that by lifting weights at the gym. You get that by pulling your child's head out of the ball return hole at a bowling alley.

DECORATION BY PROXY

I'd like to tell you an inspirational savings story about my father, John Ricker, a person I love dearly. My dad is a smart man, a thoughtful man, a hard-working man, and an honest man. He is not, however, a decadent man.

To say he's cheap is not quite right, because he's actually very generous. He's always excited to pick up the check after a dinner with his family, or randomly surprise my kids with kites he bought them at Costco. It'd be more accurate to say my dad is "vigorously practical." He hates spending money on things that seem nonsensical to him. And there are a lot of those.

For instance, he is religiously opposed to air-conditioning. I can count on one hand the number of times he allowed us to fire up the HVAC when we were kids. This policy also extends to his car, where he will not turn on the AC under any circumstances because it "uses too much gas." Instead he rolls down all the windows, even on the freeway, which is so noisy it requires everyone to yell at the top of their lungs for the duration of the drive.

He once stayed at my sister's house and neglected to bring toiletries. Instead of going out to buy a one dollar bottle of travel body wash or asking my sister if she had any to spare, he washed his entire body with the hand soap in the bathroom because "It's soap, isn't it?"

My mom threw away a pair of his old boxer shorts because they were literally disintegrating. He discovered them in the large outdoor trash can, rescued them, and continued wearing them for years to come. (FYI: You are allowed to use the Purgatory Cabinet on your husband.)

To skirt some "insurance nonsense," my dad asked a podiatrist if she would give him an off-the-books foot surgery if he paid in cash. The podiatrist actually agreed, and my dad was very proud to report she "threw in the other foot for free."

And instead of buying a nice sailing jacket he'd had his eye on, he bought a used one on eBay for fifty dollars. It was shipped in a scented garbage bag, arrived covered in stains, and when he put it on for the first time, he found a condom in the pocket. He still wears it even though it doesn't fit (the jacket, not the condom).

My dad's been like this my whole life, and his thriftiness was always most on display during holidays. For Halloween he'd just throw a couple pumpkins on the porch. On the Fourth of July we were only allowed to watch *other* kids play with fireworks, which he told us was just as fun (it wasn't). At Christmas, my childhood home would have the obligatory tree, but that was *it*. No lights, no snow globes, no animatronic Santa on the roof. From the curb, we were Jewish.

So an interesting creative challenge arose each year when it was time to take our annual Christmas card photo. My parents would want a wintery picture of us kids, but in our home the halls were decidedly un-decked. Plus we didn't live within close proximity to any snow-covered landscapes, and my dad sure as hell wasn't going to approve the cost of a trip to the Sears portrait studio.

But in December of 1994, my father hatched a plot so diabolically frugal that it guaranteed him a spot in the Dad Discount Hall of Fame, and I'm printing it here so you can become a disciple of his ways.

That fateful afternoon, my dad dressed me and my siblings

up in matching red turtlenecks, but instead of loading us into his Chevy Blazer, he gestured toward the end of our cul-de-sac and hustled us over to one of our neighbors' homes. We had never actually met these people (we didn't even know their names), but their house was by far the most festive on the block. They had a bunch of wooden cutouts of elves and reindeer, a full-on nativity scene.... They'd even covered their grass with white sheets to make it look like it had snowed. They'd spent hundreds of dollars and countless man-hours bringing holiday cheer to Danberry Drive, and these suckers were about to be grifted by the Rickers.

What happened next can only be described as the yuletide equivalent of house squatting. My dad told us to stand in front of their home and discreetly snapped our picture. It was *fine*, but he wasn't satisfied. We had just been standing on the sidewalk in front of the house, and based on that framing it was obvious what we were up to. He'd need to be bolder. "Go up on the lawn," he whispered. So we did. Three smiling children, trespassing for Jesus.

My dad's gambit paid off. It was reckless, but he got his prize. We now had a Christmas card photo that made it look as if we had decorated our *own* house for the holidays, and the only thing it cost my dad was the film in his camera and the respect of his children. So if you're looking to save money during the holidays, remember my father's teachings: Don't *buy* decorations when you can just walk *by* them. And never send Christmas cards to your neighbors.

Our first crime!

TAKE THE "EXTRA" OUT OF "EXTRACURRICULARS"

Hobbies are an important part of every kid's development, and I would never suggest you cut them out entirely. But your child joining an extracurricular activity can feel like your wallet's been diagnosed with a terminal illness: It's something you'll have to live with for years that will gradually deplete you of all resources and motor functions. You need to buy leotards, tubas, orange slices, lacrosse sticks that cost $300 for some reason—you're strong-armed into paying travel costs and membership fees, and good luck if your kid wants to do something like horseback riding. Then suddenly you're working overtime to buy groceries for your family and salt licks for a Clydesdale.

A report from Lending Tree reveals the average annual cost of extracurriculars is close to $1000 *per child*. A full 62 percent of parents in that survey say they've been "stressed" about being able to afford these activities, and 42 percent have even gone into debt to pay for them. All this so your kid can participate in something that they, let's be honest, are neither good at nor enjoy.

Some parents do this because they think it will lead to a future career for their children, but let's really play that out. Say your kid is able to parlay his Pop Warner football experience into a job as a running back for the LA Chargers making a million dollars a year. (He's not *going* to, but let's *say* it.) A million dollars a year is a lot of money, but most running backs only last three years in the league. That means after taxes he'll bring home around $1.5 million for his *entire football career.* That's not enough for a twenty-seven-year-old retiree to live on for the rest of his life! You will have given up thousands of dollars and hundreds of weekends so your kid could buy a condo in Burbank and half a MINI Cooper.

But if you *insist* on making your kids well-rounded, let's at least make their hobbies affordable. Here's a list of kid pursuits that are cheap *and* minimally entertaining!

AUDIT A SOCCER GAME

The yearly cost of being on a soccer team is around $500 per child, but that number can rocket up to $10,000 if they're in an elite club. And, with all due respect, fuck that. However, your kid can get the full youth sports experience for free if you equip them with a low-cost Amazon soccer jersey and a high tolerance for shame. Instead of enrolling your child in one of these pricey leagues, you're going to have them *audit* a game like a college class. Just take them to a random soccer field dressed to play, and when the time is right, tell them to bolt out into a game already in progress and start kickin'. They won't know any of the rules, but have you ever seen a bunch of four-year-olds play soccer? The whole game is just two exasperated coaches yelling, "Jesus guys, no hands! NO HANDS!" This chaos will provide the perfect cover for your child and allow them to spend ten glorious minutes feeling like a mini–Zlatan Ibrahimovic with a runny nose. Halftime will be the most difficult part to navigate, as it will give the rest of the team an opportunity to say "Hey, who's that kid and his dad who are sucking down all our applesauce pouches?" At that point, you and your child should run like hell, which you will have the energy to do on account of all the applesauce.

RAT CATCHING

The 1800s introduced many innovations that altered the course of human history: the lightbulb, the stethoscope, that bike with the humongous front wheel and tiny back wheel that everyone still rides to this day.... But a lesser-known Victorian-era creation called "rat catching" could be your kid's next inexpensive pastime. This is true: In large nineteenth-century cities like London that were overrun by vermin, children were paid to track down rats and kill them, which they were absolutely *fantastic* at. This makes sense, because if there are two things kids are genetically engineered to do they're "seek" and "smash." What's that you say? This is an activity no modern child would dare participate in? Well, let me introduce you to the kids of New Zealand's Stewart Island, who *in 2022* made their community safer for kiwi birds by catching six hundred rats in just over three months (sixty of which were caught by a single five-year-old!). They loved it too, because to a child, hunting rats is basically just a game of *Pokémon GO* where all the Pokémon have the hantavirus. And the best part is, the cost to become a professional rat assassin is literally nothing. All they need is a big stick and a can-squish attitude!

MINI-MIME

The performing arts give kids a chance to develop public speaking skills, explore their creativity, and, once they're in high school theater, dry hump in a prop closet. But when you account for costumes, sets, and makeup, putting on big productions can be quite expensive, and those costs are often subsidized by the actors. That's why you're going to get your kid into a performance style that's 100 percent imaginary (which is another word for "free"). Behold, the breathtaking savings of mime: one of the world's most beloved and annoying art forms. It involves a performer—often a grown man who has applied face paint in the shattered selfie camera of his iPhone 4—pulling make-believe ropes with a level of showmanship that implies we should think it is difficult. Using nothing but his mind's eye, the mime creates a whole universe without the benefit of words, scenery, or health care. And while adult mimes can look like the personification of human loneliness, child mimes can be quite adorable. So paint your kid's face and plop them on a street corner where they can act like they're stuck in a box the whole damn day. When they eventually complain about being bored, just shush them and say, "Mimes don't talk."

NOTE: Any professional or semiprofessional mimes moved to silently cry with balled fists as a result of the comments made herein by the author may receive a formal apology by sending a self-addressed imaginary envelope to:

Invisible Building
6834 Pretend Avenue
Hogwarts, Arkansas 90210

LITTLE DICK'S LEAGUE

One of the most expensive parts of your child playing a sport is all the accoutrement you have to purchase, but what if you never actually had to purchase it at all? Well you won't need to if you're willing to trick a Dick's. With over 850 locations, Dick's Sporting Goods is the largest sports equipment retailer in the continental United States. Each of their massive stores is brimming with state-of-the art gear customers can pick up, take a few practice swings with... heck, maybe even *use* if they're quiet enough to fly under the radar. Yes, with careful planning and an industrious spirit, you can form a no-cost underground baseball league right under Dick's nose. On opening day, assemble all interested kids in the parking lot and have them casually stroll into the store a few at a time as to not arouse suspicion. Each child should "try on" a uniform, then meet in Aisle Six to grab bats, balls, bases, and mitts. When it's time to start the game things will get dicey since you can't let the store's security guards hear what you're up to. Fortunately baseball already has its own kooky sign language, which will allow your child and their teammates to play the entire game in complete silence (like mimes who are actually *doing* something with their lives!). Once all innings have been played, dump the gently used equipment into a big pile on the floor and *fucking ghost*. If things go well and your league starts to grow, you can even start playing crosstown rivals like the squatter team from Big 5.

(Also during my research I discovered that the man who founded Dick's Sporting Goods was a guy named Dick Stack. That fact has no relevance to what we're discussing, but I felt it was my duty to tell you.)

JOIN A CULT

Purpose. Belonging. A sense of community. These are the reasons you're told your child should join an overpriced field hockey league. But you can get all those benefits for free, plus the promise of secrets to the universe revealed, by getting your kid onto one of the world's oldest types of teams: a doomsday cult. First of all, cults are hotter than ever. Last year, more than 98 percent of all original programming produced by Netflix was about cults. (Honestly, if your cult *hasn't* been chronicled by a streaming docuseries, it's time to take a hard look in the mirror.) You also can't argue with the savings (and the *goofs!*) a cult can bring: Room and board are paid for, matching robes and tactical urban combat classes are provided, not to mention FREE KOOL-AID and enough powdered beef to last an entire holy war! Plus your kid's days will be packed with exciting activities that serve to honor their *new* Father: the High Priest Lawrence Beauregard. Okay yes, a few years ago he was an adult virgin named Larry who worked as a shift manager at Kinko's. But one night while he was sorting the binder clips, God informed Larry he is actually the Supreme Inquisitor of the Cosmos, which means this guy is going places! Joining his merry band of disciples is a great way for your child to make friendships that will last a lifetime, as well as the next several lifetimes once the space angel Shurazu teleports them in his multidimensional radon cube to the Zorian Galaxy, home world of our Star Mother, keeper of all Level 10–aligned souls. All hail Shurazu. All hail Larry.

Hobbies teach our kids to work hard and accomplish their goals, plus data shows they can reduce levels of anxiety and depression. But other data shows that buying a ten-year-old scuba gear fucking sucks. So while you're definitely going to end up paying *some* extracurricular costs for your children, you should mitigate them as much as possible. Or you could just pray your kid turns out to be a boring lump with no personality or interests. That happened to me as a child and it saved my parents *a ton.*

THE STORE-BRAND CHILD

It's not just extracurriculars that cost an obscene amount. The price of parenting really adds up when you have to buy kid essentials like food, clothing, and medicine (or as I call them, "the Three *P*'s"—pizza, pants, and pills). But there are plenty of savings on these items hiding in plain sight . . . usually just to the left of the merchandise your children actually want, with slightly different packaging and a rip-off name that just barely skirts the watchful eye of copyright lawyers.

I'm speaking of the parent's greatest financial ally: the "store-brand" item. On average these almost-as-good goods are 25 percent cheaper than their big-name counterparts, and those are savings that can really compound over time. Plus what they lack in prestige, they make up for in practicality, which children famously love just as much! Here's a diagram on how to start saving money today by raising a discount kid.

1. Hydrox Cookies (Just like Oreos, but with a name that sounds like an industrial floor cleaner.)

2. Walgreens brand Nice! Cola (A word no one has ever said when handed this soda.)

3. "LOS ANGELES" shirt that was purchased from the clothing aisle at CVS (Three sizes too big so she can "grow into it" by the time she's in her mid-thirties.)

4. CVS bag from aforementioned shirt purchase, now doubling as a free backpack (This will cause your child to be bullied at school, which will build character.)

5. Pants from school Lost and Found box (If that other kid lost his pants, he didn't deserve them in the first place, now did he?)

6. Haircut given at home with Dad's beard trimmer (Fourteen dollars plus tip? No thanks, "Fantastic" Sam.)

7. Drugstore "reader" glasses (They're not the most stylish, nor her prescription, but they *are* $3.99.)

8. Extension cord belt (Holds up her pants, and in a pinch will allow her to use a circular saw up to twenty-five feet away from an electrical outlet.)

9. Free hat from when you won a pie-eating contest (If your kid is sporting a beard trimmer haircut, this will also cover her bald spot.)

10. Casio watch you bought with 2,500 arcade tickets from Dave & Buster's (Give it to her now, even though it was going to be the majority of her inheritance.)

11. Used shoes from Goodwill (The price of these shoes was to die for, which is fitting because the previous owner died while wearing them.)

Your kid might *look* like shit, but you know what they smell like? Money. *Your* money. And when they're eventually old enough to get their own job? That's when they can start paying the extra three bucks a bag for real Cheetos, instead of the more affordable option you've been buying: "Orange Styrofoam Puffs Featuring Horny Cheetah Coke Dealer."

EAT, PRAY, SAVE

Some parents go to great lengths to cook high-quality food for their children, but at some point you have to ask yourself, "Why should I spend a fortune creating organic meals for a person who would eat an unwrapped Jolly Rancher out of a shoe?" So we're going to give up. To embrace our kids' culinary chaos. To indulge their basic-bitch palates and save countless dollars in the process. Here are some delicious recipes that cost almost nothing to make and will be inhaled by even the pickiest of eaters.

HOT DOG CRUNCH

INGREDIENTS: One hot dog, thirty Cheerios

NUTRITIONAL FACTS: Compound nitrates delivered in a hot pork torpedo

COST: 57¢

RECIPE: This meal combines kids' favorite meat log (hot dogs) with the closest thing they have to dog food (Cheerios). First, slide a single, sad wiener out of the package, microwave it for exactly twelve seconds (just long enough to make it "sweat"), then roll it on a bed of fresh Cheerios. The warm meat secretions will act as an adhesive that sticks the cereal to the exterior casing of the sausage like little carbohydrate barnacles. Since this dish combines foodstuffs from both breakfast and dinner, you can give your kid this festive mix of whole grains and pig snout any time of day. Drizzle with ketchup, serve with a side of dunking milk, and be treated like Wolfgang Puck the rest of the day.

FRUIT ROLL-UP ROLL-UP

INGREDIENTS: One hundred Fruit Roll-Ups (unfurled)

NUTRITIONAL FACTS: High levels of maltodextrin, which is . . . food?

COST: $22 (serves fifteen to thirty kids, depending on how thin you slice it)

RECIPE: Kids love Fruit Roll-Ups because they take something they like (fruit) and minimize all the vitamins, minerals, fiber, and fruit. While these edible floor tiles are filled with a number of tasty flavors from the essential food group known as SYNTHETIC FRUIT-THEMED COMPOUNDS, they just aren't that filling. So for this recipe, carefully unroll a hundred individual Fruit Roll-Ups, stack them on a lightly floured surface, then knead this unholy mass of food coloring into a high-fructose corn boulder. Wrap it in a layer of Fruit by the Foot to increase structural integrity, then carve it up for the kids like it's a prime rib at the HomeTown Buffet. Gravy is not required, but it is, as always, encouraged.

DENTED CAN OF ELMO BEANS

INGREDIENTS: 55 oz. can of beans

NUTRITIONAL FACTS: Low

COST: Even lower

RECIPE: Beans are one of the cheapest foods in the world, but it's hard to get kids to eat them because they're not *thrilling.* Fortunately, children are suckers for nonsensical product integrations. Most kids don't want to wear Pull-Ups, but get ones with Iron Man on the crotch and they can't wait to urinate on their favorite Avenger. Your daughter always fought you about brushing her teeth, but now she loves using her tube of Crest featuring a completely unrelated picture of Belle from *Beauty and the Beast.* (Belle lived in a rural eighteenth-century French village without running water. No way ya girl brushed her teeth.) You're going to use the same psychological game here to serve your kids a dirt-cheap dinner, one that may even be cheaper than eating dirt itself. Go to your local grocery store and head straight to the back. You're looking for an off-balance plastic bookshelf with a sign that says "Manager's Specials" (it's usually right next to, and sometimes even inside, the employee bathroom). This display will be brimming with products approaching their expiration dates that the FDA has deemed technically fit for human consumption, which is grocery speak for "great deal!" Rifle through its contents until you find a dented can of beans (there's always a dented can of beans) with a cartoon character on it. Your options will be limited; you might have to settle for a third-tier *SpongeBob* character, or a cartoon bear from a South American country you've never heard of, but if you're lucky you'll score an A-lister like Elmo. When you get home, just pop the top, hand your kid a spoon, and encourage them to eat their weight in baked beans, *just* like Elmo always does.

GO-TATOES

INGREDIENTS: Potato

NUTRITIONAL FACTS: Potato

COST: The cost of a potato

RECIPE: One of the best kids' foods ever is mashed pota-toes. They're inexpensive, easily produced in bulk, and your children can't wait to pack 'em thick into every inch of their little arteries. But we can all agree the #1 prob-lem with mashed potatoes is they're impossible to eat while skateboarding. So taking inspiration from the cur-rent king of tubed food (Go-Gurt), Go-Tatoes combine the convenience of food pouches with the rich, starchy flavors of Ireland's most cherished root vegetable. Simply make a massive batch of mashed potatoes and funnel them into discarded Otter Pop sleeves. You can also add bacon and chives to create a variety of flavors, or freeze them to eat fifty years from now after World Wars III and IV.

FUCK-IT NUGGETS

INGREDIENTS: Ugh

NUTRITIONAL FACTS: Not great

COST: At this point, who gives a shit

RECIPE: It's 10 p.m. It took you three hours to drive home from the carnival and your children are suffering from starvation-induced assholery. They begged you for something called "deep-fried spaghetti" before you left the fair, but you took a stand, refusing to pay forty dollars for that culinary hate crime against Italians. Now your kids' blood sugar has crashed and if they don't eat immediately, they will violently implode. Unfortunately they're shooting down every food of remote nutritional value, so you're gonna have to set aside all your good parenting instincts and deploy the nuclear option: Fuck-It Nuggets. This is a dish that should only be made in emergencies, since it is likely to cause irreparable damage to any internal organs it rubs up against, but it's both cheap and effective so

Here.

We.

Go.

First, pull out your biggest mixing bowl and tell the kids they can fill it with any ten food items from the kitchen. Deli ham, raisins, sprinkles, pancake batter...The only rule is that they need to do it *fast*. Once the bowl is filled with this demonic concoction, mix it with an immersion blender, then frantically stamp it into shapes with some Christmas cookie cutters. Preheat the oven to nine hundred degrees and bake for a count of "Three Mississippi" (you don't have the luxury for anything longer than that). Let the kids get second-degree mouth burns as they quickly eat their shame, then it's off to bed for eight excruciating hours of indigestion.

Ultimately food is fuel, and there's no need to fill your kids up with the fancy stuff. Is this healthy? My heavens, no. If a forty-year-old ate like this they'd be dead in a week. But children's bodies are resilient and scorch calories with the intensity of an imploding star. And while they *may* develop scurvy on this diet, that'll just bring them one step closer to becoming one of those pirates they love so much!

BEFRIEND A RICHER KID

When I was growing up, my family's existence was solidly middle-class. We lived in a small house my parents purchased for $119,000, our vacations never involved flying on airplanes or staying in nice hotels—but none of that mattered to me. My happy little life was simple, practical, measured, and modest. Except for the one weekend a month when I rolled like a fucking billionaire.

I got to do this because my best friend at the time, a preschool classmate named Bret, was quite rich. His parents owned a successful meat distribution company, so their family had what I can only describe as *beef wealth*. When we met, Bret lived in a three-story house on the beach, which was actually his family's starter home. (A few years later they moved to a house that had a private dock for their yacht, which was some real Tyler Perry shit.) Bret was a great friend and his family treated me as one of their own, regularly letting me sleep over and tag along on luxurious boating trips to Catalina Island off the coast of LA. In fact, it was on their boat that I experienced the fanciest thing any kid in the '90s could possibly imagine: We watched a VHS copy of *Home Alone* . . . at sea!

Before Bret and I became friends, it had never even occurred to me that some people had more money than others, but I remember the specific moment I understood the concept of tax brackets. It was on Halloween 1989 when Bret and I both dressed as Batman.

That's Bret on the left in a Batman suit that rivals the actual Batman's suit: cape, cowl, utility belt, outerwear underwear, and some officially licensed slip-on Bat-Vans. Then there's me, sporting a Batman T-shirt, sweatpants, an overgrown mullet, and an expression that says, "I realize now that I am just wearing pajamas."

But the financial dynamics of our dynamic duo didn't bother me one bit. I wasn't ashamed my family had less than his, plus Bret owned a Super Nintendo, Nerf guns, top-shelf Ghostbusters toys, and I got to play with them all. My preschool best friend had become my sugar daddy and my parents didn't have to pay a dime to support my newfound taste for the finer things.

So how does this apply to you? Obviously a genuine cross-caste friendship like Bret's and mine is rare, but you could *synthetically* create a similar arrangement for your child if you're willing to find them companionship using cold-hearted capitalism and a little elbow grease. Follow me here.

Every year *Forbes* magazine puts out a list of the richest people in the world. Scan those names looking for any potential connection you may have with these titans of industry. Perhaps you share a love of hiking with Bill Gates, or maybe your grandpa is from the same part of hell as Rupert Murdoch—work all angles. Once you pick your one-percenter, research if they have any offspring who are the same age as your kid and start playing millionaire matchmaker. This *will* require you to rent your child an ascot and sneak them into a few Met Galas, Grand Prix, presidential fundraisers, what have you. But they'll be fine as long as they know what to say when the rich kids ask what their favorite Swiss bank is.

Once your child makes friends with a wealthy heir, they'll assume a role similar to those young women who "fall madly in love" with an oil tycoon in a wheelchair during the last six weeks of his life, or one of the many strange men with chinstrap beards who have married Britney Spears. They're there for the expense account. To use that trust fund for some trust *fun*. And yes your kid may be called a gold digger, but guess what gold diggers get. *The gold.*

Some of you may be saying, "This feels gross. I don't want my child to take advantage of someone just because they're rich." And you're right. You're clearly an ethical person (must be nice!), but there *is* still a way to pull this off while keeping your conscience completely clean. Yes, just like Robin Hood, you and your kid can go straight to the top of the *Forbes* list to embezzle money from the most controversial and beloathed businessman of all time.

The richest person in the world (as of this writing) is Elon Musk. He owns (as of this writing) Twitter, Tesla, and SpaceX. He has not (as of this writing) brought about the downfall of modern civilization, but has (as of this writing) eleven children, some of whom still (as of this writing) speak to him. He is the Nick Cannon of megalomaniac billionaires, and if you're doing the math, eleven kids gives your child a lot of potential opportunities for high-end, all-inclusive playdates. Just think of it: Instead of having to pay for your child to go to the arcade like a commoner, they could be shooting flamethrowers in zero gravity with a kid named Xa%2[Bryan], or running hugely popular social media sites into the ground then pretending they did it on purpose! And because you are their legal guardian, you'll get some fringe benefits too: like becoming friendly with Elon's army of AI Tesla-bots so they won't harvest *all* your organs in the coming techno-apocalypse.

It's always better to be playing with house money, so why

not let your children play with the money of a guy whose house is a giant skull carved into the side of a volcano (as of this writing)? Admittedly, this plan is a long shot, but a wise man once said, "When something is important enough, you do it even if the odds are not in your favor." That man was Elon Musk, and what could be more important in this life than that zany douche flying your family to Saint Barts to glamp in a yurt?

THE COLLEGE SAVINGS APTITUDE TEST

The price of college has more than doubled in the twenty-first century. Today, the average cost for the average university to educate your (truthfully, below average) kid is over $100,000. And that number can soar even higher if your child wants to attend a private school, double-major, or eat.

Most parents have to start saving for this massive expense while their kid is still in utero, which can get tricky. College funds like a 529 plan offer great tax benefits, but you're forced to spend the money you put into them on education. So what happens if you save in one of these for eighteen years, but then at the last minute your kid decides he wants to become a ferry-boat captain, or skip college altogether to start an OnlyFans for his feet?

I've solved this problem with a quiz I call the CSAT (College Savings Aptitude Test). In just fifteen questions, I can determine which level of higher education your child will seek based on their current behavioral trends. Keep score as we go and I'll tell you exactly how much you need to save.

1. At least once a week my child . . .
    (A) Takes piano, cello, or sitar lessons [4 points]
    (B) Creates art using a variety of mediums [3 points]
    (C) Drinks from the toilet (tank) [2 points]
    (D) Drinks from the toilet (bowl) [1 point]

2. I would describe my child as ...
    (A) Astute, diligent, and innovative [4 points]
    (B) Resourceful, clever, and dexterous [3 points]
    (C) Streetwise, like a stray cat or car thief [2 points]
    (D) Kevin, because that's his name [1 point]

3. My child's favorite subject to learn about is ...
    (A) Impressionist art and its impacts on consumer culture [4 points]
    (B) Trigonometry [3 points]
    (C) Birds [2 points]
    (D) Dead birds/hitting dead birds with sticks [1 point]

4. If my child was given a chemistry set, she would ...
    (A) Carefully follow the instructions [4 points]
    (B) Pour various chemicals in a beaker to see what happens [3 points]
    (C) Pour various chemicals on the dog to see what happens [2 points]
    (D) Get caught up in a whole Walter White–type ordeal [1 point]

5. The superhero my child identifies with the most is ...
    (A) Superman: courageous and strong [4 points]
    (B) Wonder Woman: honest and compassionate [3 points]
    (C) Wolverine: hairy and stabby [2 points]
    (D) Thor: hates his brother, hits people with an old hammer [1 point]

6. My child's proudest accomplishment is . . .
    (A) Learning to play Beethoven's 5th [4 points]
    (B) Making honor roll [3 points]
    (C) The fact that she's never eaten a carrot [2 points]
    (D) The time she barfed in a rental car so bad that I had
        to rent another rental car [1 point]

7. When my child prepares for a test, he . . .
    (A) Studies diligently for weeks [4 points]
    (B) Pulls an all-nighter [3 points]
    (C) Claims the test is rigged and lawyers up [2 points]
    (D) Buys clean urine on Craigslist [1 point]

8. My child reads . . .
    (A) Above her grade level [4 points]
    (B) At her grade level [3 points]
    (C) Nothing, because we live in a state where the act of
        reading has been outlawed entirely to ensure books
        don't turn our kids bisexual [2 points]
    (D) *USA TODAY* [1 point]

9. When my child grows up, she would make a great . . .
    (A) Doctor: studious and empathetic [4 points]
    (B) Photographer: artistic with an eye for natural beauty
        [3 points]
    (C) Hollywood agent: loves lying, especially for money
        [2 points]
    (D) Zookeeper: owns a shovel, can handle a good bitin'
        [1 point]

10. My child consumes culture through . . .

 (A) Monthly trips to local museums [4 points]

 (B) Frequenting the theater [3 points]

 (C) Watching online videos of *other* kids going to museums and theaters [2 points]

 (D) The time he guessed my Hulu password and watched every film in the *Fifty Shades of Grey* Cinematic Fuck-a-verse [1 point]

11. If my child got lost in the woods, she would . . .

 (A) Use geography and star positions to navigate a way home [4 points]

 (B) Build a shelter out of her surroundings to survive the night [3 points]

 (C) Join a family of wolves, then complain the whole time that the wolves were not paying enough attention to her [2 points]

 (D) Start a forest fire because that's what Smokey Bear said to do. Or was it *prevent* forest fires? Doesn't matter. Fire time [1 point]

12. My child's main priority is . . .

 (A) His education [4 points]

 (B) Helping others [3 points]

 (C) Consuming over three thousand calories a day in refined carbohydrates [2 points]

 (D) Showing all his haters that HE'S the baddest bitch in the third grade [1 point]

13. My child has written...
    (A) A number of award-winning short stories [4 points]
    (B) A play that was performed at her school [3 points]
    (C) The word *vagina* on my car in permanent marker [2 points]
    (D) A lengthy manifesto explaining why she stormed the Capitol [1 point]

14. My child's primary hobby is...
    (A) Athletics [4 points]
    (B) The arts [3 points]
    (C) Testing the limits of human patience [2 points]
    (D) Watching YouTube while casually tugging on his penis [1 point]

15. This last one is visual. Show your child the drawing below and ask them what they see.

   Did they answer...
   (A) "Microorganism" [4 points]
   (B) "Sun" [3 points]
   (C) "Hairy pizza" [2 points]
   (D) "Butthole" [1 point]

RESULTS

Okay, have your kid's score? Let's calculate how much you need to sock away for your little genius and/or Kevin.

46–60 POINTS: YOUR KID'S GOING TO A PRIVATE UNIVERSITY!

Good news! I have terrible news! You need to save around $250,000 for your kid's education. This will allow them to spend four unbelievably expensive years studying things they could have probably learned for free on TikTok. While sending your child to this school will completely wipe out your retirement fund, they will always have a period of their life when they ate all their meals in an old wooden dining hall that looks like where Harry Potter had his bar mitzvah, and can you really put a price on that? (You can. It's $250,000.)

31–45 POINTS: YOUR KID'S GOING TO A STATE UNIVERSITY!

Whew, you only need to save a measly $40,000 for your child's education. State schools may not have the pizzazz of private universities, but they get the job done and don't ask for much in return. They're Arby's, Amazon Prime Video, a state-accredited Ross Dress for Less. They're the guy you settle down with; sure he's bald and unambitious, but he'll never cheat on you (mostly because no one's interested in him, but he also thinks having an affair sounds like a lot of work). And with the money you'll save sending your kid to Adequate State, you can add an additional room onto your house for when they move back in with you immediately upon graduation.

21-30 POINTS: YOUR KID'S GOING TO A COMMUNITY COLLEGE!

Ah, community college. Daycare for adults. Your child will have many interesting experiences here, like giving five dollars to a homeless person on their first day of school, only to discover minutes later that man is actually their civics professor. You'll need to save around $5,000 for your child's education, but they could also get all the benefits of community college for free through something I call the "Liars Scholarship." This is where you just claim you went to city college even though you did not, and no employer is willing to spend the thirty seconds it would take to confirm it.

20 POINTS OR BELOW: YOUR KID'S GOING TO BE A SOCIAL MEDIA INFLUENCER!

You need to save $0 for your child's education. All things considered, this is probably your best-case scenario. When it comes to college, not only will your kid cost you literally nothing, but there are big money-making opportunities to be had. Instead of your child pissing away eight years learning how to be a podiatrist, they'll be honing their craft: filming themselves opening various products and saying "OMG wow!" As their fame grows, you can name yourself their talent manager, skim 10 percent off the top, and buy a motorcycle your spouse will get in your inevitable divorce. Sure, your child's career as an Instagram huckster will tear your family apart at the seams, replacing your once-happy existence with a bloodthirst for "likes" and "favs," but that . . . is the end of this sentence.

Here's a quick personal story to prove the importance of this exam. When I was in college, I lived on the same dorm floor as a pre-med student whose name I will redact. This young man's parents were paying a lot of money so their son could study microbiology, but he instead chose to fill his semesters with decidedly less scholastic endeavors, like cutting a hole in his window screen that he could smoke/pee out of (he lived on the seventh floor, above an open-air quad). He also acquired a brick of weed from Mexico that he sold from his bunk bed, burned all his nipple hair off with a cigarette lighter, and once got so drunk he passed out in front of me with a piping-hot cup of Top Ramen spilled on his bare chest. It may shock you to learn that this man did not end up going into the field of medicine, and if only the CSAT had existed back then, right now his parents could be popping wheelies in a high-end Winnebago. So before you start gambling your life's savings on that kid who's sitting naked in your favorite chair picking their nose with a french fry, just try to determine whether they're going to end up a Steve Hawking or a Steve-O.

COST-SAVING ADVENTURES IN BABYSITTING

$15,000 a year. That's how much daycare can cost you in many parts of America. And babysitting is quite the scam when you think about it. Any time my wife and I want to leave the house alone, we're required to pay hundreds of dollars so our kids can be presided over by a lesser adult? One who eats our food, messes up our Netflix algorithm, and sits on our couch making out with her boyfriend Zayden, who we don't think is right for her *at all*?

But steep childcare discounts are all around you if you can bend the norms of society to your will! Here's how to get your babies sat on a budget.

IT'S FREE-A AT IKEA

Ikea stores have a large indoor playground/babysitting area called Småland, a Swedish word meaning "to take advantage of a large furniture retailer." This is a free service to customers, and they don't even interrogate you about whether you're actually there to purchase a cardboard dining table. According to Ikea's website, Småland features "various play facilities for children" where they can enjoy "ball pools, coloring, play with a range of Ikea children's toys, and watch movies and animations in the cozy place." While leaving your kid with a stranger to "watch animations in the cozy place" should normally raise a number of red flags, this is Ikea . . . inventors of the KALLAX shelf unit! The only speed bump here is that there's a one-hour time limit on their childcare, but that should be plenty of time to admire some four-dollar rugs in peace and take a quick work Zoom from their home office wing. Plus Ikea's babysitting services can be used *once a day*, which means annually you can reap 365 free hours of that world-famous Scandinavian hospitality.

COST: $0.

ADDED BENEFITS: Tiny meatballs.

POSSIBLE DOWNSIDES: Angry Swedes.

LEAVE YOUR KID AT WORK DAY

Many businesses have a "Take Your Kid to Work Day," when children are encouraged to visit the office and witness first-hand how truly depressing their parents' lives have become. But this melancholy core memory for your kids can also be used as an annual opportunity for eight hours of no-cost childcare. Bring your kid into the office that morning, sit them down in your Soviet-era cubicle with the sticky Dell computer, then say, "Welp, I gotta cut out early. Can you cover for me?" Your child will *jump* at the chance to do grown-up office work (because they're too young to understand the crushing weight bureaucracy has on the human spirit), and you'll be free to drive home and watch *Bridgerton* in your underwear. Your child will be safe (you've worked there twelve years and nothing *remotely* exciting has ever happened), and hey, maybe they'll make friends with Darren from accounts payable because he *also* likes anime and never stops talking.

COST: $65 to buy your kid a 5T power suit.

ADDED BENEFITS: Unlike when you do it, if your child falls asleep in a meeting everyone will just say "Awwwwww!"

POSSIBLE DOWNSIDES: Your child could actually be really good at your job, get promoted, and then you are dealing with a whole Boss Baby thing.

DON'T LET THEM NOT GET STUCK IN A CLAW MACHINE

There are a few unalienable patterns of nature: Birds fly south for the winter, cicadas emerge on a tight timetable, and babies get trapped in claw machines. That's not a joke, it happens constantly. Here's just a sampling of the news coverage on this recurring phenomenon:

Firefighters Rescue Yet Another Child Stuck in Claw Machine (Global News, 2019)

Why Do Toddlers Keep Getting Stuck inside Prize Machines? (Yahoo, 2018)

Children Climb into 'Claw Machines' More Often Than You Might Think (The Legal Examiner, 2012)

There Is a Kids-Stuck-in-Claw-Machines Epidemic (Gothamist, 2014)

That's right, an epidemic that can save you *tons* of money.

It makes sense why kids climb into these things: They have flashing lights, fun music, and are brimming with prizes, like an infant's version of Caesars Palace. So if you hang around an arcade long enough, your child's guaranteed to scuttle on up that chute, where they'll be completely protected inside a Plexiglass cube and cushioned by the pile of stuffed Pikachus

that have been there since 1997. All I'm saying is, when this inevitably happens, maybe don't *rush* to alert the staff. Go grab a coffee, take a few laps around the mall, *then* call the fire department to break them out.

COST: Roll of quarters to rescue them.

ADDED BENEFITS: A picture of this will do *great* on your Instagram.

POSSIBLE DOWNSIDES: Another kid might win your kid.

JESUS SAVES

Many churches have Sunday school, which is a weekly class where children can learn the teachings of Christ from an adult virgin in a polo shirt. This is often provided free of charge during the main church service, for even the Lord knows your kid won't sit through a two-hour sermon on the power of prayer. But what if instead of heading into the chapel after dropping your kid at Sunday school, you *hypothetically* bolted back to the car and sped away for a guilt-ridden but child-free morning alone? I mean, everyone honors the miracle of creation in their own way, and maybe yours is getting a break from the screaming little miracles *you* created.

You don't even need to be a Christian for this to work, by the way. In fact, it's best if you're not religious at all. Atheists don't have to worry about the Ten Commandments for the same reason box turtles don't have to worry about the tax code; it's a set of rules that has no jurisdiction over them. Granted, if it turns out God *does* exist you are going to be in a ton of trouble, and will likely spend the rest of time getting your ass poked by pitchforks. But since your kid is now a disciple, at least one day they'll get to play volleyball in Heaven with Abraham Lincoln and the Skipper from *Gilligan's Island*.

COST: Your soul.

ADDED BENEFITS: Your child becomes a moral person, which you are not.

POSSIBLE DOWNSIDES: Eternal damnation (but only if real!).

HOLLYWOOD!

This is the only babysitting method out there that will actually *make* you money, and it's easy too! Step 1 is to get your child a job as a famous actor. Doesn't need to be anything fancy, maybe a supporting part in a Steven Spielberg film, or a role playing the quirky child of Kevin James on a CBS sitcom that runs for nine seasons yet somehow is not watched by a single person you've ever met. Step 2 is to lean back while the checks roll in and let an army of production assistants tend to your child's every need. In "the biz," as horrible people call it, a whole team of professionals are hired to watch child actors like a hawk. There are producers making sure kids only work certain hours, studio teachers doing fake schoolwork with them between takes, craft service chefs stuffing them full of Bagel Bites, and all of these individuals are, technically speaking, babysitting your little star *for free.* The age of your child dictates just how much studio-funded childcare you can get for them: Older kids can work almost a full day, while babies under six months can only work for twenty minutes at a time. But that'll be long enough for you to squeeze in a nap while a film crew slathers your infant with goo and pretends to birth them from the nether regions of Jennifer Lawrence.

COST: Negative millions of dollars.

ADDED BENEFITS: Your child might get a highly merchandisable catchphrase like "Mamma mia, that's a spicy lasagna!" (It doesn't have to be that exact phrase, but that one's gonna be hard to beat.)

POSSIBLE DOWNSIDES: None. Every child actor grows up to be a well-adjusted adult.

They say it takes a village to raise a child, and I feel the same way about childcare. Why not make your kid *everybody's* problem? If you can do that, you'll never again have to pay two hundred bucks for a babysitter to lounge around your house while Zayden drinks all your Diet Dr Pepper. (Ugh, fucking Zayden.)

THE TRASH HOUSE PROTOCOL

We spend a lot of money protecting our home from fire, floods, earthquakes, and thieves. Yet we do nothing to safeguard it from destructive child forces who attack it from the *inside*, like lupus personified. That's probably because it feels like a losing battle; the woeful truth is that you'll never be able to stop your kids from trashing your house, *but what if your house was trash to begin with?*

That's the philosophy behind my most aggressively frugal parenting technique: the Trash House Protocol. To use it, all you have to do is find the shittiest living quarters you can, then reside there for several decades until your youngest child becomes an adult and moves far, far away. Maybe it's a shipping container at an abandoned meatpacking facility, or a rickety old brothel haunted by the ghost of the Mafia don who was murdered there. The point is, you should not waste money on a home you want to be "nice" or "clean" or "inhabitable," because your kids will see to it that none of those goals are ever achieved. It's the same reason you wouldn't drive a Lamborghini in a demolition derby: You're gonna lose $300,000 *real* quick.

My wife and I adopted this approach as a matter of necessity. Every night we (through hours of exasperated begging) get our kids to clean up all their toys. Our objective is that by the time the kids are asleep, someone walking into our home would never know we have children. We get there most nights, but then by 6 a.m. the next morning our house looks like this:

We pay thousands of dollars a month to live here.

Each day our house is hit with an unceasing barrage of friendly fire. Floorboards are splintered. Carpets are defiled. Smoothies are detonated. Our kids are basically the Property Brothers, except they're a pair of siblings who *decrease* the value of our home. That's why you must initiate the Trash House Protocol, which requires you follow just three simple rules.

RULE 1: NEVER BUY NICE THINGS

You work hard to put food on the table (food that is then smeared all over that table). You tell yourself that you *deserve* nice things, and you do. But you can't have them. Not yet.

Many times over the past few years, my wife and I have thought about moving to a better place, or at the very least buying a new piece of furniture. But we know deep in our bones that within ten minutes of committing an act of such arrogance, the item would be dented, scratched, filthy, or aflame—a way for the Parenting Gods to punish our hubris. We now debate every prospective home update by gaming out how quickly our children will destroy it. I imagine it's the same conversation the military has when deciding if a Humvee is fit for combat: "It *looks* good, but can it withstand a blast from a roadside bomb?" With kids the answer is often no, and that forces you to make some compromises.

I don't know why, but I've always wanted that symbolic "nice home" decor item: the large vase with fancy sticks in it. Whenever you see one of those fuckers in someone's house, you're like, "Woah, this dude is *rich*." But I can't have one, because I know at the end of its first day in our home, the vase will be shattered and my kids will have jammed the sticks in each other's eyes. So instead we settled for a consolation tchotchke: a single, unassuming decorative basket for our living room. Small, gray, wicker. Our hope was that it was so boring, it'd be invisible to our children's Destructo-Vision. But much like how a caterpillar transforms into a cocoon, which transforms into a silk moth—that decorative basket transformed into a make-believe hot-air balloon, which then transformed into a broken decorative basket.

We are also in desperate need of a new couch, but we know it'd be irresponsible to get one based on the indignities our current sofa has endured. It has been begrimed with urine, stool, snot, blood, barf, and milk (both cow and human), plus it's covered in a light dusting of every cracker known to man, which gives it the consistency of a damp crouton. It's also where our houseguests are forced to sleep, which seems like a health code violation on our part. It would be more hygienic if we forced my mother-in-law to sleep on the bathroom floor of our local Denny's.

We even tried to update the closet in our bedroom, a small but useful home upgrade we figured the kids wouldn't even think to mess with. And yet within a few days, they turned our new shoe rack into a half-eaten pancake museum.

A childless person would call an exterminator over this.

So if you *do* happen upon the oversize stick vase of your dreams, go ahead and buy it. That's your goddamn right. Just remember to swaddle it in Bubble Wrap and hide it for years until the day your last kid leaves for college. Once the coast is clear, bring your *new* bundle of joy down from the attic, when it will be able to sit freely in your dining room without being karate kicked into oblivion.

RULE 2: GIVE YOUR KIDS A "RUIN ROOM"

If you have any chance of keeping your common spaces clean, you need to give your kids one area of the house they can just annihilate with garbage. This is called a "controlled explosion," like when police confiscate a shipment of illegal fireworks and blow it up in a field. The space you let your kids ruin can be a corner of the living room, a patch of dirt in the side yard, maybe that spot under the house where you hear raccoons fighting at night. For our family, it's our kids' nightstands. Even if we ask them to clean their rooms, the nightstands are allowed to go untouched; we give those diplomatic immunity like an international embassy for their shit. Here is what my daughter has chosen to keep within arm's reach while she sleeps.

1. Nutcracker
2. Landline telephone
3. Handpainted unicorn
4. Cutout of potato chip bag
5. Bottlecap
6. Doll clothes
7. Hospital hairbrush from when she was born
8. Empty roll of tape
9. Broken crayons
10. Baby spoon
11. Bowl of cherry tomatoes
12. Framed photo of our friend's cat

Sometimes just to help myself let this go, I pretend it's an art installation called *Gary Busey's Earthquake Kit*.

Whichever part of your home you designate the "Ruin Room," be smart about its design. As Founding Father (and, again, certified *freak*) Benjamin Franklin once said: "An ounce of prevention is worth a pound of cure." So cover the floors with rubber mats like a horse stable. Install a drain in the center so you can hose it down. Line the walls with sheets of plastic like one of Dexter Morgan's kill rooms. Do whatever it'll take to make cleanup easy, because when your nest is eventually empty, you're going to do what a landlord does after they evict a bad tenant: Rip out the carpet, spray for roaches, and finally put down those new hardwood floors you've been having sex dreams about.

RULE 3: LIVE THE TRASH LIFE PROTOCOL

The beautiful part of the Trash House Protocol is that it can be expanded into all other areas of your life as a parent, because there are hundreds of other things you should not spend significant money on until your kids are grown. On top of a trash house, you should have a . . .

TRASH CAR: Don't lease a Lexus or you'll be changing blown-out diapers on your NuLuxe leather seats.

TRASH WARDROBE: Don't wear Versace jeans because the pockets will be filled with partially eaten lollipops your kids "want to save for later."

TRASH PHONE: Don't buy the nicest iPhone. It's just going to become a sticky brick your kids use to play Roblox.

TRASH BODY: Don't spend money on pricey exercise

equipment. No amount of dumbbell curls will reverse the fact that you stress-ate a tube of Pringles for dinner. TRASH BRAIN: Don't spend money on therapy just yet. Eventually it will be a powerful tool, but right now your kids can counteract even the best therapist with a simple comment like "Your second chin has a zit."

To save real money you've got to tear not just your house, but your *whole damn life* down to the studs. If you don't, your kids will happily do it for you. So your mission, should you choose to accept it, is to live the next portion of your life like Donnie Wahlberg—the reliable, discount Wahlberg. You're not in Martin Scorsese films. You don't sleep in a cryo chamber. You're just using your remaining New Kids on the Block royalties to fly yourself coach to the grand openings of various Wahlbergers franchises. But hold your head high, keep at it, and one day when your kids are grown, you'll finally be able to upgrade your life from "Donnie Economy" to "Marky Mark Medallion" status.

UPDATE:

Between the time I originally wrote this chapter and when I came back for revisions, my wife and I did something incredibly stupid. Ignoring our own advice, we moved to a new house and bought some nicer furniture. I say without exaggeration that on day one, our son threw a new ottoman across the room and shattered a glass picture frame.

UPDATE TO THE UPDATE:

Between when I wrote that first update and when I am writing this updated update, our son also smeared bright pink slime on our new curtains because he "thought it'd be funny."

We have realized the error in our ways and are moving our family into the sewers like the clown from *It*.

MILLION-DOLLAR IDEAS: MONEY-SAVER EDITION

Let's wrap up this section on money with some inventions that will save you some (and again, save *me* some, when you design and manufacture these, then send me one for free).

KID BLINDERS

Because everyone who has ever designed a theme park, zoo, or museum is a giant dick, you cannot exit any of these establishments without walking your child through a gift shop (or as I call them, "inconvenience stores"). These enraging spaces are filled with "souvenirs" your children claim they need to "remember" the trip, which may be the most sinister marketing tactic ever unleashed on parents. The idea that your child, who complained nonstop throughout this entire visit to the Grand Canyon, needs a stuffed coyote to wistfully reminisce about it for years to come is truly absurd. Most times we take our kids someplace, the whole family agrees we should never speak of it ever again, so why the fuck are we buying mementos? This is where Kid Blinders come in. These are modified horse blinders, which are typically used to block the peripheral vision of racehorses and keep them focused only on what's ahead. You, however, will strap them on your kid's head so you can leave this aquarium without having to pay $39.99 for a back scratcher shaped like a moray eel.

FOOD GLUE

On average, kids only eat 50 percent of the meals you make them, and that number drops to a staggering 6 percent when you've overpaid for that meal at a restaurant. It's hard to watch the busboy take away your child's plate and not think, "There goes $9.50 in uneaten grilled cheese." But from now on your kid won't waste a single bite of grub with Food Glue, a one-of-a-kind edible paste that adheres half-nibbled cheeseburgers, quesadillas, ravioli, et al. into all-new Franken-entrées. This will save you hundreds of dollars a year, and also allow your child to experience exciting new flavor profiles like Flamin' Hot Peanut Butter and Bologna Alfredo.

"NEW TOY!" PACKAGING

There are many times when your child spends months claiming they *need* a specific toy, only to finally get it and completely lose interest an hour later. As birthdays and gifting holidays roll by, their room gets hit with waves of hard plastics they quickly become blind to, but you can get your kid

re-excited about a toy they totally forgot they own with "New Toy!" Packaging. This looks just like the box a new toy would come home in from the store, complete with plastic window, phrases that oversell the item, and even those little black zip ties that feel like a prank on people with arthritis. Place a toy you bought your child years ago inside this box, then watch them tear it open while experiencing a potent mix of materialistic euphoria and chilling déjà vu.

LAP CHILD STADIUM SEATING

Flying with your kids costs an insane amount of money, especially when you have to buy them each their own dandruff-dusted airplane seat. But you can enjoy mile-high savings by taking advantage of a glaring loophole in an airline's lap child policy. "Lap child" is a designation given to small kids who can fly for free as long as they're sitting on their parent's lap. Usually a parent can only accommodate one lap child because Mother Nature only *gave* us one lap, but with Lap Child Stadium Seating you'll outsmart three billion years of evolution *and* a JetBlue flight crew. This is a tiered seating system similar to what you see in hockey arenas, which will give you enough laps to accommodate your entire brood. Stack your kids up vertically (putting the least barfy one up top) and work out a snack-passing system like a bucket brigade or *The Human Centipede*. (I never saw that movie but assume this is an apt comparison. No spoilers please.) If you're feeling bold, shove your husband up there too and claim he's a "lap spouse."

KIDDIE LITTER BOX

Diapers and wipes cost hundreds of dollars a year. Kitty litter is $8.99 at PetSmart. You can choose what you do with that information.

OKAY, SO NOW
YOU'RE RICH . . .

YOU ARE CRUSHING THIS. You're now saving money on your kids' food, clothing, childcare, hobbies, and education. Soon your 401(k) will be flush and you'll be able to buy that set of grillz you've had your eye on (the tasteful ones with diamonds that spell out "PIMP"). There's just one problem: You can't *use* all your new-found time and money, because you're a total fucking nutcase.

There is one final step to you becoming a person again, a fully realized adult able to dreamwalk in both the world of parenting and the realm of the living. We need to dive deep into the darkness and retrieve something you lost long ago, at the exact instant your first child came umbilical cord bungee jumping into your life.

Let's funnel some sane back into that brain.

PART III

Your Mind

My son. He does this thing.

When he finishes his dinner, he walks over to my side of the table, grabs the arm I am eating with, and shakes it vigorously until the food falls off my fork. This bothers me on a molecular level. I mean, on one hand it looks hilarious, like something Larry would do to Shemp on *The Three Stooges*. But on the other hand, it feels like some kind of alpha male caveman shit.

I don't know why he does it. I don't think *he* knows why he does it. But he does it—and there is something so elemental and primal about my child, whom I have dedicated my entire life to, flailing my arm so hard I can't even get a bite of macaroni in my mouth. That's a small example of the challenges parents face, but it's emblematic of what we're all up against here: psychological warfare. An assault on *our very minds.*

The "mind" is an interesting concept. It's not your brain per se—that's just a squishy organ filled with neurotransmitters and a detailed list of every time you've said something awkward at a party. No, your mind is more amorphous than that. It's your personality, your spirit, your aspirations. All the things your kid shook off your metaphorical fork the second they were born. That's why if you're ever going to become a real person again, your mind must be protected, preserved, repaired, and fortified.

In the final section of this book, I will teach you to calm your emotions, even your keel, rebuke prepubescent gaslighters, and come to peace with the realities of your situation in an attempt to achieve just an ounce of zen amongst the whirlpool of kid chaos you find yourself drowning in. I'll also recount my biggest victories and most embarrassing defeats as a parent, then make a revolutionary call to action that just might save the holidays for us once and for all. We're almost home. (And thankfully not *your* home. That's where all those screaming kids are.)

THE STUFFED ANIMAL BILL OF RIGHTS

It's Christmas Eve. 4 a.m. You're trying to load your family into the airport shuttle waiting outside and you're already twenty minutes late. You finally get everybody buckled in when your five-year-old announces you cannot leave. "Why? Are you sick? Do you have advanced knowledge of some sort of terror plot at the airport?" No, she says, you forgot something: a sweater for Cheety, her stuffed cheetah. You dismiss her request as you climb into the Sprinter van with the impatient driver, but your daughter starts to weep. How could you be such a coldhearted monster? This cheetah is now guaranteed to get frostbite on your half-hour flight to Tucson, and she's a member of your *family*.

No she's not, you explain. She also doesn't need a sweater because she has fur, you explain. And they don't *make* tiny sweaters for cheetahs, you explain. Plus Cheety doesn't have nerve endings, so she can't experience the sensations of heat and cold, you explain. "But Cheety will DIE!" your daughter explains. So back in the house you go to fashion a miniature cardigan out of an old sock. This story is (slightly) fictional, but it could happen to you if you make the same misguided decision I did of granting civil rights to your child's stuffed animals.

My daughter has always been a #StuffyMom. At various points in her life, her menagerie of "children" has included:

- The aforementioned Cheety the Cheetah
- Tootsie (penguin)
- Chicky (chicken)
- Foxler (fox)
- Mr. Meow (cat)
- Pusheen (fat cat)
- Bella (fluffy cat)
- Blueberry (blue cat)
- Ralph (black cat)
- Courtney (marshmallow cat)
- Disinterested (grumpy cat)
- Lucky (ceramic cat)
- Lucky 2 (identical to Lucky 1, who was lost at the park)
- The Grinch (man with . . . terrible disease?)
- A porg from *Star Wars: The Last Jedi* (which eventually looked like a dirty owl)
- And "Skeleton Adele" (a plastic Halloween decoration she snuggled with for an entire fall season until all its lead paint rubbed off on her face)

It's sweet the first time your kid personifies a toy and cares for it. "What an imagination! They're so compassionate! Maybe they're not a total sociopath after all!" But be warned:

This is a trap. While it's tempting to play along, the moment you recognize a stuffed animal as an equal is the moment your life becomes dominated by that fiber-filled fucker. The stuffy will soon start requiring its own special sleeping arrangements, it will develop opinions you're expected to consider, and you'll suddenly become the caregiver, personal assistant, and private chef to a completely inanimate object. "Oh, Plushy Puppy doesn't like strawberry jelly, he only likes *grape* jelly? Why, what a refined palate for someone whose mouth is a piece of string!"

Because we didn't shut this situation down in our house, things began to escalate. When our daughter was six, she informed us that Mr. Meow's birthday was coming up in three days. We said, "We can't wait!" and completely blew it off, but she continued the countdown.

"Mr. Meow's birthday is in two days, what do we have planned?!"

"Mr. Meow's birthday is tomorrow, did you buy a cake?"

Only then did we realize our daughter was not letting this go and we were in an impossible position. It was 9 p.m. on a Tuesday, did we need to go to Party City and buy balloons for a terrycloth cat? We elected not to, and the shit hit the fan.

"Mr. Meow can't be sad, it's his SPECIAL DAY!"

"We can't leave Mr. Meow alone on his BIRTHDAY!"

Needless to say, we were then forced to make Mr. Meow's birthday one he would never forget. Even though he lacks the ability to remember things. Because his head is a cotton ball.

Having not learned our lesson, we got that same kid a Tamagotchi, the popular '90s "virtual pet" that's made a nostalgia play in recent years. It's a plastic egg with a little black-and-white creature on the screen. You have to feed it, play with it, and clean up its pixelated poop (which was what we considered fun back before the internet existed). And if you don't care for it properly, your Tamagotchi beeps loudly and dies, like a pager that gives you guilt.

When our daughter went to school she tasked us with caring for this electronic critter, which we foolishly agreed to. We could have just said, "We're not going to do that, because we have jobs and that is a toy," but instead we gushed, "We'd *love* to babysit for you!"—which led to us getting forced into servitude as full-time Tamagotchi nannies. As our daughter walked out the door, she gave us a number of condescending instructions, like a parent leaving her newborn with a couple of inexperienced teenagers.

"If he's bored, you need to play a game!"

"He eats hamburgers and candy, but not too much!"

Unfortunately, as soon as the Tamagotchi was placed in our custody, it digitally defecated—so we (two college-educated adults) were forced to spend a long while trying to figure out which intricate series of button presses would pick it up. We eventually gave up, which caused the Tamagotchi to shuffle off this mortal coil. And when our daughter returned home to the news of its death, she sobbed—much more so than I believe she would cry if I were to die. We then had to devote our afternoon to consoling her like a grieving widow.

A few months later the Tamagotchi (having been reincarnated hundreds of times) went on a hike with us. I begged for it to stay behind, but my daughter shot me an incredulous look and said, "You want to leave your grandchild in the CAR?!" It came with us, of course, but at the end of our walk she realized she had dropped the Tamagotchi somewhere along the trail. I just wanted to go, but had a teary-eyed kid glaring at me saying, "You want to leave your grandchild in the WOODS?!" So out I went, to search for an 8-bit frog amongst the leaves like I was Mariska Hargitay in a very stupid episode of *Law and Order: SVU*.

Learn from my follies. To ensure your mental energy is dedicated to the well-being of your kids and not every goddamn toy in your house, you must draft a comprehensive constitution and have it ratified by all members of your family: adult, child, and stuffed. Here's a template.

THE STUFFED ANIMAL BILL OF RIGHTS

- *Unless you were birthed, you do not get a birthday party.*

- *Food will only be served to those with a small intestine.*

- *If instead of a heart you have one of those flat watch batteries, you do not get to decide where the family goes on vacation.*

- *You will not receive an allowance if you have a lower back tattoo that says "MADE IN CHINA."*

- *Characters in iPad games do not get in-app clothes purchases. I did not drive my real car to my real job to make real money so I could buy a fake scarf for an imaginary squirrel.*

- *You cannot be "sick" if your immune system is made of polysynthetic fibers.*

- *If your eyes are buttons, you do not get a shout-out in our bedtime prayers.*

- *You cannot receive Christmas presents if you yourself were once a Christmas present.*

- *And should you get lost, no search party will be launched if an exact replica of you can be purchased at Target for less than twenty-five dollars.*

This document will be the bedrock of your newfound sanity. If you're ever going to regain enough personal focus to floss your own teeth, you can't also be planning a quinceañera for a Furby. Let's work on getting civil rights sorted out for women and people of color and the LGBTQIA+ community, and then, *maybe*, circle back to Mr. Meow.

PRETEND YOU'RE IN CHARGE

I'm going to tell you something frightening, but it's important that you hear it: Your power as a parent is completely imaginary. You're only in charge because your kids *assume* you're in charge. Since the moment they burst from your loins, you've been there, keeping them alive and knowing how to do shit.

You're also only in charge because *you* assume you're in charge. How could you not be? Look how much bigger you are than this squishy baby, who would literally choke if you didn't mince his grapes into tiny little pieces! But this dominion over your kids is but smoke and mirrors. It is a house of cards that can fall at any moment, and you have likely taken this very tenuous arrangement for granted.

There will come a moment in your child's life when they realize you're not actually an all-knowing deity, but just some random doofus who fell into the job. They'll come to understand you're more of a royal figurehead. (And not even a good one like the Queen; you're one of those third-tier royals like the Duchess of Frumpletits.) It will feel similar to the first time you got pulled over by a cop who was younger than you: Your kid will look at you with indignation and think, "Wait, *this* fucking guy's telling *me* what to do?" And then it's game over.

This crumbling of parental control is often due to a lack of training. There are classes on how to birth your children and give them CPR, but there are no courses on how to keep them in line, which means every parent has to figure out this very nuanced process in the heat of the moment. Case in point: No parent knows what's going to happen the first time they "count to three." When our children misbehave we start counting at them in a stern tone, because *we* were sternly counted at when *we* were children. But then you suddenly find yourself shouting numbers at a toddler with no solid game plan, and it dawns on you that this whole thing is subterfuge.

ONE . . .   *(Oh no, she's still not picking up her toys.)*

TWO . . .   *(Oh shit . . . I better come up with a good punishment.)*

THREE . . . *We're going to dress you up as Guy Fieri for Halloween!*

The system has failed you, but I'm here to help. You must never loosen the iron grip you have on your household, because the second the kids smell blood in the water they'll topple your regime like a statue of Robert E. Lee. And while you may not actually *have* power, you can certainly *project* it. Here are some ways to sell the big lie.

INSIST THEY HAVE AN OLDER SIBLING YOU PUT BEHIND BARS

Whenever your kid is disobeying you, casually drop a comment like "Wow, you're acting *a lot* like Dylan right now" or "This is *exactly* the kind of thing that got Dylan caught." When they ask who Dylan is, reply, "Your older brother Dylan. . . . You don't remember him? He *also* used to smear toothpaste on the mirror until I turned him in. He's out on parole soon, I hope you get to meet him." If they ask to see a picture of Dylan, just Google Image search "Adult Justin Bieber" and try to get a single tear to roll down your cheek.

HIRE A HEAVY

As your kids get taller, you seem less and less imposing to them. There's even that terrifying point in time when you realize, "My kid would probably kick my ass if I wasn't the one paying for the Wi-Fi." That's why you need a heavy. You've seen these guys before, either in mob films or standing behind more demure supervillains like the Riddler (who is basically a human sudoku puzzle). They are typically Italian American men who are 6' 3", 280 pounds, and brandishing a balled-up fist the size of a Christmas ham. While in the movies heavies rough up anyone who gives their employer trouble, for your purposes they're just going to repeat everything you say but in a borderline offensive New York accent. Your kids may not move when *you* tell them to brush their teeth, but imagine what they'll do when a guy who looks like Vincent D'Onofrio bellows, "You hoyd the boss! Scrub dem chompers!"

CREATE A NONSENSICAL POINT SYSTEM

Every elementary classroom in the world uses a star chart, color-tier system, or pom-pom jar as a visual representation of how well the students are behaving. Kids get *pumped* about this, and will follow every single rule for even the *possibility* of a "party" where they eat lukewarm Shakey's pizza at their desk. You can adopt a similar technique at home, but to keep yourself in the power position you're going to make the rules vague and constantly move the goalposts so it's impossible to win (just like a carnival game or working in the entertainment industry). Place a big chart on the wall and give each of your children 10 Star Points, which they'll be ecstatic about. But the first time you hear them fighting, say, "If you don't cut it out, I'm going to deduct 40,000 Star Points!" Even though being 39,990 Star Points in the hole means literally nothing, your kids will do everything they can to avoid it. Once they build up to a million Star Points, present them with an exciting business opportunity: trading them all in for a Silver Moon! They will pounce on this limited-time offer, at which point you'll explain that unfortunately right as the transaction went through, the Stars-to-Moon exchange rate plummeted and now they're basically broke. So they'll have to be *super* good for the next two and a half years to get their heads above water.

AFTER-SCOWL PROGRAM

Here's another idea from the world of education. When my kids are misbehaving, I'll often ask them, "Would you ever act like this at school?" and their reply is always "No, because I'd get in trouble from my teacher." When I explain that I am *also* an authority figure in their life, and that they are currently in trouble with *me*, they say "okay" and go right back to using my laptop as a Frisbee. That's because unlike parents, teachers hold a sacred place in a kid's hierarchy of power—somewhere between the Holy Ghost and Doctor Strange. With the snap of her finger, a teacher can make thirty wild kindergartners march in time like the North Korean military, and there's a mutually beneficial opportunity to be forged here. Everyone but the federal government seems to agree that educators are tragically underpaid, so why not recruit your kid's teacher to sit in your living room during her off-hours and glare sternly at your children? She'll make some extra cash, and your kids will do everything that's asked of them because unlike you, Mrs. Birkenkotter has the jurisdiction to make them write a ten-page report on photosynthesis.

OUTSOURCE DISCIPLINE TO A "FAMOUS" PERSON

Cameo, if you're not familiar, is a website that connects regular people to a wide array of celebrities who were not smart with their money. For the price of a party sub, you can make these financially challenged stars of yesteryear say pretty much anything you want: Dennis Rodman will congratulate you on a clear prostate exam, or the lead singer of Sugar Ray can wish you luck at your upcoming DUI trial. The future is truly upon us. And Cameo has a whole section of animated celebrities who your kids consider to be A-listers, including Thomas the Tank Engine, JJ from *CoComelon*, and the demon known as Blippi. This means you can buy a video of someone your kid reveres much more than you (a talking train) telling them to do their chores, and it will actually work! You will be thrilled at how effective this is once you get over how sad it is.

DRESS FOR THE RESPECT YOU WANT, NOT THE RESPECT YOU HAVE

I'm not trying to be rude, but you do not look tough. I can't even see you right now, but I know it to be true. After years of parenting, your muscles have liquified and your body is the shape of a yam. You also dress like an assistant librarian and no longer have the aura of someone who should be listened to, so you need to give yourself a makeover—one that's gonna let not just your kids, but *everyone* know who's the fucking boss. Hit up your local pawnshop / biker rally / swamp-boat repair depot, and outfit yourself with the following accessories that always convey an image of authority: a bandana, wraparound sunglasses, leather pants, fingerless gloves, a boomerang, an earring made of an eagle feather, a giant gold cross necklace (even though you've never cracked a Bible), a tribal tattoo (even though you were born in Vermont), a sixty-four-ounce Monster Energy jug—and top it all off with a high-fade power

BEFORE   AFTER

Hell yeah, brother. Now those are two
badasses who've got it all under control.

mullet. You'll know you're done when you feel like Mom or Dad the Bounty Hunter and look like the subject of a *Queer Eye* episode *before* the Fab Five shows up.

Okay, repeat after me:

"I run the show."

"I call the shots."

"I am an adult, who is worthy of esteem."

Good. I almost bought that. Appearances are everything, and you need to present a strong one to your kids. Never forget that parents are just middle-aged Tinker Bells, and we'll cease to exist unless the children *believe.*

CHAOS MEDITATION

The benefits of meditation are bountiful: reduced stress, increased willpower, a stronger sense of self...all things we must obtain on our quest to get our real lives back. Unfortunately, traditional meditation routines are for childless hippies whose only concern is finding gluten-reduced deodorant at the farmers market. You have mouths to feed, asses to clean, and no place you can sit in silence for three seconds without hearing the phrase "I SPILLED JELL-O IN THE DRYER!" But fear not, because we're going to bootstrap nirvana through my patented and parent-friendly zen practice known as Chaos Meditation.

I use CM any time I'm in a situation my wife and I call "commercial parents." This is when the environment our children are creating around us is so insane, it looks like we're actors playing parents in an over-the-top Olive Garden commercial. Like if we're trying to chat over dinner but our kids are pulling each other's hair, a toy whale is blaring "Row, Row, Row Your Boat," and a plate of projectile fettuccini clips one of us in the temple....that sort of thing. The key here is to completely disassociate your emotional state from your physical body, just like that one time David Blaine froze himself in a block of ice for attention.

Using this method, you can find stillness in mayhem. Calm in pandemonium. Tranquility in a Build-A-Bear Workshop. Maybe even right in this moment you're at a Mommy and Me class that's gone sideways, and you've frantically flipped to this chapter searching for solace. You're going to get through this. I promise. Just focus your chi and follow me.

(1) GET COMFORTABLE

To relax the mind you must first relax the body. It doesn't matter if you're corralling a Little League team at Wienerschnitzel or slathering your infant's undercarriage with ointment at a TSA checkpoint; do a couple quick stretches, center your balance, then slump face down on the floor like a sack of wet newspaper. Yoga has something called "Child Pose"; this is a similar position called "I've Had Enough of My Child Pose." At this stage it's important to cease all motor function. If you look dead, people won't touch you for fear of being cursed.

(2) CLOSE YOUR EYES

Next, close your eyes. Like, hard. Until you see the little spots. While normal meditation practices would have you do this gently, you can't run the risk of your kid prying your lids open to show you a worm he stepped on. Let this darkness embrace you like a warm blanket, ignore the fact that the carpet of this indoor playground smells like a sick dog, and simply "note" any sounds you hear without applying worry to them. These noises will likely include your children screaming about mozzarella sticks, and other envious parents asking why *you* get to take a floor nap. No bother. Just let these irritations pass you by, like your hairline and your chance to become a professional softball player.

(3) SENSE YOUR SENSATIONS

Slowly scan your body, identifying everything you're currently feeling. That nerve you pinched giving a horsey-back ride. Your baby sling scoliosis. The puncture wound you suffered stepping on a Polly Pocket. Kindly greet these earthly pains of the flesh, then bid them adieu as you gradually shut down your entire central nervous system. This will block all physical distractions that may hinder your enlightenment, including your sleeve being tugged, your ear getting flicked, and your asymmetrical love handles getting kicked by a plastic *Peppa Pig* sandal.

(4) BREATHE DEEPLY

Now that you are in a self-made haven of sensory deprivation, the real mental repose can begin. The urge you feel to yell, not just at your kids but at whichever maniac thought it was a good idea to put a finger-painting station at this planetarium? Suck it deeply into your lungs and slowly exhale, watching that anger dissipate into a fine mist that floats away to become one with the universe. That calm you feel? It's because you just bong-ripped your own rage.

(5) ACKNOWLEDGE WHEN YOUR MIND HAS WANDERED

While you are in this transcendental state, a number of stray thoughts from your past may bubble to the surface. Maybe even some you'd locked deep down inside:

> *Should I have devoted all my teen years to becoming an Eagle Scout, even though it became increasingly clear my neckerchief was prolonging my virginity?*

Should I have finished college instead of going on tour with my ska band—a two-week trip that put me $30,000 in debt?

Was Jake the IT guy actually hitting on me at the Christmas party that one year? And if I hadn't brushed him off that night, would we currently be married and living in the beachside compound he built after selling his "Tinder for dogs" start-up for $3.6 billion? And if so, would I still currently be playing possum on the floor of this laser tag arena?

It's okay when these thoughts occur. Just imagine them as raindrops that fall from the sky, land on a palm leaf, then roll into the sea. The very same sea you and Jake could be tearin' up on a Jet Ski right now.

(6) WAKE THE FUCK UP

While most mindfulness practices would tenderly bring you back to consciousness, you don't have time for that new age nonsense because you're at a roller rink where your kid is pinned under an air hockey table. So defibrillate your mind and come hurtling out of your trance with the concussive force of a neutron bomb. While the duration of your session may have been brief, Chaos Meditation operates outside the laws of physics and time functions differently down there. Sometimes just a few moments of CM can feel like years, which will likely be enough to get you through the remainder of this Minions-themed fun run.

(7) TEMPORARILY REGAIN SANITY

Hey, what's different about you? Did you get a blowout? Lose some weight? Hold on, I know what it is: You have that small flicker of life back behind your eyes. We just straightened out a figurative paper clip, stuck it in that tiny hole in your soul, and gave your brain a factory reset. While you are already back dealing with the atrocities of the Legoland food court, you just transported to an astral plane of parental respite you never thought possible, and now you can visit it anytime for a quick brush with serenity. *Brush with Serenity* is also probably the name of the yacht rich Jake could be railing you on right now. Ugh.

Namaste.

THE DRUNKEST HOUR

Once you're responsible for the well-being of children, you quickly realize you need to curb your insatiable thirst for booze, weed, mushrooms, and anything else you might find jostling around in Willie Nelson's fanny pack. But that's *also* the time you really need them, because taking care of kids is life's most simultaneously stressful and boring activity (even more so than teaching your dad how to store his photos in the cloud).

It's critical that your children have a parent who's coherent, present, and engaged. But it's also well within your rights to have a small, time-appropriate, chemically induced trip to the dark side of the moon. I've devoted a lot of personal research and development to this particular topic, and there are exactly five instances when it's okay for parents to get a little buzz going. Again, I'm not saying you *should* do this. I'm saying you're *allowed to*. According to *me*.

ANY CARTOON CHARACTER'S LIVE SHOW

At some point in recent years, all your child's most beloved and annoying cartoon characters have made the jump from the small screen to a full-blown theater production. *Barney Live! Baby Shark Live! Curious George Live!* . . . poetically, all shows that make the parent chaperones wish they were

dead. But not anymore! Because now when you agree to take your kid to a musical where a major media conglomerate's intellectual property is dancing around on roller skates, you'll earn the right to have thirty-two ounces of your favorite domestic beer or one fully charged vape pen. This should also help you forget that you paid a week's salary to attend something called *The Kidz Bop Never Stop Tour*.

LITERALLY THE SECOND THEY GO TO BED

They say when you have children, the years are short but the days are long. Most days even *feel* like a year, so the final moments before your kids go to bed can have all the excitement of watching the ball drop on New Year's Eve. That's cause for celebration, but planning ahead is key because you don't have long before you yourself pass out like a pig on a hot rock. So when their little heads hit the pillow, you need to be ready to *rage*. Limes must be cut, ice buckets must be filled, and you should come flying out of your kid's room at Usain Bolt–level speeds. Sometimes while my wife is reading a book to the kids, I'll silently hold up a bottle of wine in her eyeline like an undercover sommelier, just so she knows she's got a triple-pour of Pinot when it's go-time. And the best news is, the whir of your child's white noise machine will blend seamlessly with the sounds of you spraying booze all over your kitchen like a team that just won the World Series.

AT A PLAYDATE WHERE THE OTHER KID'S PARENT IS AN ATOMIC WEIRDO

When your kids start making friends of their own, one of three scenarios arise:

SCENARIO 1: The kids get along, the parents are awesome, and everyone loves hanging out. (This almost never happens.)

SCENARIO 2: The kids don't like each other, but the parents are the coolest people you've ever met, so you force the children into friendship like an arranged marriage. (This never works.)

SCENARIO 3: The kids become *best* friends, but the parents are awkward mole people who have seemingly never had a conversation with another adult. (This, unfortunately, is 98 percent of the time.)

When you find yourself in this third situation, getting your families together can feel like a terrible first date on a polygamist hook-up app. After you and the other parents have discussed such riveting topics as the weather and what size shoe everyone wears, it is A-OK to whisper the phrase "I brought some gin." Even if the other parents don't drink gin (they don't), you go right ahead and have yourself some gin.

A SCHOOL PLAY YOUR CHILD ISN'T EVEN FUCKING IN

You thought you dodged a bullet when your kid didn't audition for the school play, but then something even worse happened: Their friends *did,* and now your child's demanding the whole family watch six-year-olds you've never met play dancing monkeys in a knock-off *Wizard of Oz.* When *your* kid is in a terrible play, it's adorable. You gloss over the subpar acting, singing, choreography, costuming, and stage presence because you're wearing Parental Pride Goggles. But when you don't have a dog in the fight, the entire performance feels like a back-alley root canal. And school plays are not known for their brevity. I once went to one of these where after ninety minutes (and a musical number that felt like it had to be the grand finale), the principal grabbed the mic and announced we'd reached *intermission*. It was the first time I'd felt an entire theater sigh. Not the audience, but the building itself. So from now on, the person who hands out the little xeroxed programs should also ask if your child will be on stage that night. If you say no, they'll hand you a White Claw and a lit cigarette.

DAYLIGHT SAVING DAY

The worst two days of the year for parents are the second Sunday in March and the first Sunday in November: our mount and dismount from Daylight Saving Time. The United States adopted DST in 1918 (a time in history when only good decisions were made) in an attempt to conserve energy. And yet over a century later, its only remaining purpose is to take energy *away* from parents when it turns our children into werewolves every few months. Even though the clocks only move an hour, our kids wake up like little Han Solos getting unfrozen from carbonite: in shivering wet lumps on the floor shouting "I can't see! What year is it?!" Daylight Saving infects kids with something I call "the Madness": that insane energy that comes from nowhere and lasts for weeks. If you go to any park in America the day after the clocks change, every kid will be running ripshit around the playground with their shirts off while every parent stands there despondent and mumbling, "What the fuck just happened?" So I'm lobbying to make the day after Daylight Saving a drinking holiday like Cinco de Mayo, but specifically for people with kids. That day will go down a lot easier if you're sipping a margarita from a giant novelty clock cup hanging around your neck.

Again, safety and discretion are of the utmost importance here. Don't do something stupid like consuming an irresponsible amount around your children. But *also* don't do something stupid like going to their school's all-night "Harry Potter Festival of Magic" without a cocktail hidden in your Yeti mug. If they're making you yell "Expecto patronum!" you can have some Patrón.

SWEARING IS CARING

Parents are forced to lead a double life. There's the version of yourself you present to your kids: the worldly, well-adjusted go-getter who enjoys artisanal salads and reading *New Yorker* articles about artisanal salads. Then there's the real version of you: the beef goblin whose only real hobby is watching skyscraper implosion videos on the commode. And the aspect of our true identities that's most taxing to hide from the little ones is our deep, enduring love of profanity.

When we're around our kids we're required to act like we've never used (or even *heard*) our favorite expletives. If they tell us one of their classmates said the B-word, our response is supposed to be "Oh my gosh, *what*? There's a B-word now?!" even though we know full well we've used that term to describe every single member of our pickleball league. Keeping up this charade is exhausting because it requires a real-time rendering process—one where we must constantly scan our mental thesaurus for bubbly, kid-friendly alternatives to phrases like "motherfucker" and "shit bird."

So for your own sanity, I'm granting you a waiver that will give back a significant portion of your cerebral bandwidth: From now on, you can curse in front of your kids, and your kids can curse in front of you. I know this feels strange, but it's going to be okay. I have scientific proof.

One of my dearest friends in the world is a woman named Ruby Brown. She is a loving, compassionate, well-read mother of two who graduated with a degree in English from UCLA. She also happens to talk like Tony Soprano if he got his dick slammed in a car door. I've known Ruby more than half my life and am still nervous to be with her in public due to the volume (amount and decibels) of her Olympic-level swearing. At restaurants I'll often hide behind my brunch menu as Ruby loudly declares her least favorite member of the royal family a "bald, pink snatch."

When our families both had our first child in 2014, I asked Ruby if she was going to stop talking like Scarface getting an unmedicated colonoscopy and her answer was a hearty "FUCK no." I personally decided to take the G-rated approach with my kids, so an interesting social experiment began: My home was the control subject, and Ruby would find out what happens when your family is written and directed by Quentin Tarantino.

Ruby and her husband (my other dear friend Mike) said every curse word imaginable in front of their two young children, and by the time their boys were in kindergarten they were both completely over it. Yes, these kids knew the forbidden words—but they also knew when it was inappropriate to use them so it never became an issue. Ruby and Mike didn't have to expend energy policing language in their house, and their boys were more mature because of it. Meanwhile, my wife and I were raising our kids down on *Sesame Street* and it was causing some unsettling side effects.

For instance, when our daughter was two I needed to reference a certain part of her anatomy during a lesson in hygiene, but I didn't know which word to use. "Butt" describes the entire area, "anus" is too scientific, and "fanny" is horrifying. What I really needed to say was "butthole," which was far too crass to teach a child. However that word *could* be shortened into something more palatable, so I went with what I thought was the most wholesome option: B-hole. My daughter misheard me though, and started calling that particular orifice her "beagle." My wife and I thought it was funny, so we let it ride.

Flash forward to five years later: In the name of modesty we had still never corrected this charming error, and our daughter had conflated things even further. She now thought "beagle" meant "penis" and had taught that to her three-year-old brother, who was running around naked saying it every chance he got. So I was forced to intervene, and because I had been so intent on my kids not hearing a bad word, I now had to sit them down for a family meeting and explain the following:

1. A "beagle" is not a penis, it's a butt.
2. The term isn't actually "beagle." It's "B-hole," which you probably shouldn't say.
3. "B-hole" is short for "butthole," which you *definitely* shouldn't say.
4. If you hear Auntie Ruby say "asshole," that means butthole. Also, don't say anything Auntie Ruby says.

I had finally set the record straight, but my little speech brought *a lot* of attention to this word, and things only got worse from there. Once my kids learned about "butthole," they found it to be deeply hilarious (which, in their defense, it is), and this plunged our family cursing policy into uncharted waters. That's because "butthole" is not a curse word per se; it's a *naughty* word. Kids love saying these because they're getting away with something, but the act does not rise to the level of punishment (see also: *wiener, ding-dong, dumper,* and *toot chute*). Suddenly dozens of times per day in our home, "butthole" would be shouted, sung, or even drawn, like when my children collaborated on this beautiful Andy War-hole.

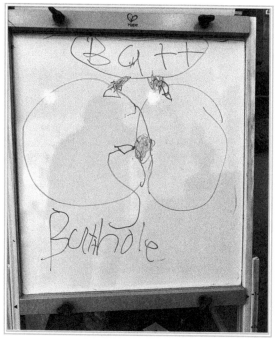

If you can't tell, one of them drew a butt, and for biological accuracy, the other one added the hole. And in case *that* wasn't clear enough, they labeled both the "butt" and "butthole," then drew arrows to them. (This is the kind of attention to detail our family prides itself on.) Now my reluctance to say this one word one time had metastasized into an ongoing crisis in my home—*and* a classy art collection!

So why are we doing this? No . . . why the *fuck* are we doing this? We're so worried about our kids hearing this short list of evil words that we're walking around pretending to be members of the Mormon Tabernacle Choir. Bad words are only "bad" because *we* assigned that value to them. Imbuing these random collections of syllables with dark connotations only makes them more tantalizing to kids. Plus our children understand social nuance way more than we give them credit for. In fact, they themselves live a double life: At school they're kind and obedient scholars dedicated to furthering their education; at home they're feral hogs who bite each other for the iPad.

So if you step on a Hot Wheels car, it's okay to yell "goddammit." If your kid spills their milk and says "shit"? Everything's going to be all right. You can spend your every waking moment regulating your home like the FCC, or you can do as Ruby did: Just raise a couple of HBO kids and call it a day.

Speaking of Ruby, she gave me some words of wisdom to end this chapter, which I have turned into a motivational poster you can hang in your home. Enjoy.

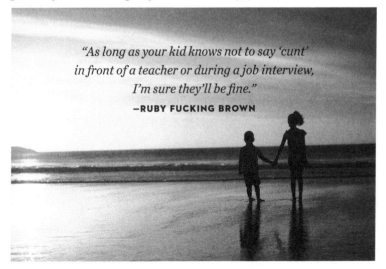

"As long as your kid knows not to say 'cunt' in front of a teacher or during a job interview, I'm sure they'll be fine."
—RUBY FUCKING BROWN

THE 7 MOST HIGHLY EFFECTIVE LIES TO TELL YOUR KIDS

Your kids lie to you about literally everything. They *did*, in fact, whip their sibling with a pool noodle. They *did not*, in fact, wash their hair this month. They *do*, in fact, remember what happened at school today—but good luck getting it out of them, ya old hag. Some days the fibs get so frequent you feel like the detective in an Agatha Christie novel, deciphering a twisted web of deceit to determine which child put your car keys in the toaster. It's maddening, but there's a reason your kids lie so much: because *it fuckin' works*. They can get away with anything because their fundamental lack of empathy allows them to stare you dead in the eye and make up some truly crazy shit.

We, however, are not allowed to lie to *them*? This amazing tool that can solve any problem is off-limits to us because we're supposed to be more mature than our kids? Not in my house. I believe deeply that just because you're the *physically* bigger person doesn't mean you need to be the morally bigger one too. We are under siege here, and we need to fight liar with liar.

After experimenting with these extensively on my own children, I have assembled what I believe are the seven most highly effective lies to tell your kids. This is not a joke. Each one of these has changed my life in its own special way and tipped the scales of insanity back in my favor. They're about to do the same for you—please use them both responsibly and often.

LIE #1: THAT YOUR CAR DOES NOT PLAY KID MUSIC

Kid music is the pride of the Devil. It's reductive, repetitive, and often sung by a strange man who's tinkling a xylophone while whispering about itsy-bitsy spiders (which, if you ask me, sounds like something from the twisted mind of Stephen King). Or sometimes the music your kids like is actually kinda *good*, but they've forced you to listen to it so many times that any song from the *Moana* soundtrack now kicks you into a state of fight-or-flight, which is just an unsafe condition to be in behind the wheel. But you can exile all *Encanto* sing-alongs from your SUV with this simple little lie: Tell your kids from an early age that all cars lack the ability to play kid music. Same way you can't watch Netflix on the microwave; it's just not wired to do so. Explain it's because of a software compatibility issue having to do with microchips and electrical currents—and even though that's not remotely true, really go in-depth. Just like when tech support starts telling you what an IP address is, your kids' eyes will glaze over and they'll just pray you stop talking.

I'm telling you, this works. No single lie I've told my children has benefited me more than this one. And even if your kids don't buy it initially, it's okay, because they're physically restrained in the backseat (per the law!) and you're the only one who can reach the stereo. So . . . sorry kids, you *can't* listen to the Wiggles, but you *can* enjoy the soothing sounds of this fantasy football podcast!

LIE #2: THAT YOU ARE NOT TICKLISH

Like all respectable taxpayers, I hate being tickled. But kids *love* tickling their parents because it instantly reverses their power dynamic with you. With a couple flutters of their fingers, the person who controls every aspect of their life is instantly incapacitated on the floor. (This is also the reason America's favorite pastime is watching presidents tumble down the stairs of Air Force One.) I realized early on that I couldn't just ask my kids to not tickle me, because that would only make them want to do it more. But if I never gave them the *satisfaction* that tickling me brings, maybe they'd lose interest and wander off, like when you play dead to avoid being mauled by a grizzly bear.

So I started a rumor in our house: that I am not, nor have I ever been, ticklish. I told my kids that 12 percent of people (a completely made-up number) are physically incapable of feeling tickles and I was one of those lucky individuals. They didn't believe me at first and immediately started tickling my feet. But like a criminal trying to beat a polygraph test, I took slow breaths and kept a straight face for what was the most excruciating eight seconds of my life. After I delivered this Oscar-caliber performance, my kids walked away disappointed and I have bathed in the glory of my newfound immunity ever since. This ruse has been in effect for over three years now and I'm terrified they will read this chapter someday, because it would honestly ruin my life. If you choose to try this on your own kids, I'd probably tear this page out of the book and eat it.

LIE #3: THAT YOU'RE GOING TO "CHECK THE TAPE"

Whenever I suspect my kids are lying to me about committing some behavioral indiscretion, I say I hope they're telling me the truth because I'm about to "check the tape." Years ago I told them I installed dozens of microscopic cameras in every

room of our home and can watch footage from them on my phone at a moment's notice. These cameras are supposedly invisible to the naked eye, but record video so high definition they can see a kid sneak a single M&M from the pantry in the middle of the night. I never have any actual evidence

they've done these things of course, but when I pull up that imaginary surveillance app it's like I'm Maury Povich opening a paternity test envelope, and it's always enough to coerce a hasty confession. (To this day, they are pretty sure the smoke detectors in their bedrooms are part of my advanced spy network and I will not be correcting them.)

LIE #4: THAT YOU ARE A GENIUS/TOTAL FUCKING IDIOT

Your kids ask you thousands of questions a day. Many of them are hard to answer (like "Where does wind come from?"), while others are downright disturbing (my son once asked me the Werner Herzog–esque query "Do birds *disintegrate*?"). Responding to all these in a thoughtful, accurate way requires an unreasonable amount of brainpower, so just don't be thoughtful or accurate. Your kids' limited access to the internet makes you their de facto expert on every subject in the universe, which means you can put a quick end to any question if you lie about the answer with authority.

How big is space? Fifty feet.

What happened to velociraptors? They live underground. That's what earthquakes are.

Who invented milk? Dr. Steven Urkel.

And while this lie works well, the only problem with it is that if you pretend to be a genius, you're expected to come up with some kind of answer. So if you want to spend even less mental energy on this never-ending game of *Jeopardy!*, make your kids think you're the *opposite* of a genius (also known in the world of academia as a "Total Fucking Idiot"). That way you can stop any line of inquiry with some blunt-force stupid.

Why does it rain? Nobody knows.

What do you call a baby horse? Huh?

How do they make spaghetti? Who's "Spaghetti"?

LIE #5: THAT YOU ARE ALLERGIC TO THE THING THEY WANT

My wife and I are not really "animal people." We wish we were, but if I'm being honest we'd probably be more comfortable touching a corpse than petting a dog. So on the many occasions our kids have pitched us the idea of getting a pet, we've had to come up with a series of flimsy reasons why we can't, ranging from "We don't have enough space" to "Most hamsters are racist." But we were eventually able to put this conversation to bed with the checkmate excuse of "Mom is allergic." Which is . . . *kinda* true. My wife is, or was at one time, mildly allergic to pet dander. If we went to the house of a friend who had a cat, she'd sniffle a bit and fully recover by the time we got home. But through a stiff mix of conviction and exaggeration, we've spun this minor fur intolerance into an anaphylactic time bomb ready to explode at the mere sight of a Labrador.

You can do this with your kids too. Tell them you'd *love* to bring another living creature into the house that is somehow even more destructive, loud, and ungrateful than they are, but it's out of the question because it might make you sneeze. You can even try telling them you're allergic to nonanimal items you don't want in the house. If you're allergic to guinea pigs, there's no reason you can't also be allergic to a Nintendo Switch.

LIE #6: THAT "WE DON'T HAVE THAT IN OUR CITY"

Kids' loose grip on geography is rivaled only by their rudimentary understanding of the global supply chain, which is why a persuasive lie to use when your kids ask for something crazy is to tell them "We don't have that in our city."

"Oh, you want to spend my whole week off at a trampoline park? Sorry kiddo, our city doesn't have trampolines."

"I would gladly pay $280 a year for a streaming service called GarbageTrucks+, but our city just doesn't have it!"

"You want to see a movie called *Karate Farm 2*, an outing that will require me to spend multiple hours watching a CGI goat voiced by John Cena? Doesn't look like that's playing in our city. Or country or planet."

I know you're thinking your kid is too savvy to fall for this one, but I know it works. That's because for many years, it successfully worked on me.

When I was a child, I wanted nothing more than cable

television. All the kids at school were watching classic Nickelodeon hits like *Rugrats* and *Doug* while I was stuck with whatever fuzzy broadcast cartoons our roof antenna could pull out of the sky. I begged my parents to pony up that extra thirty bucks a month, but instead of saying no, which would have resulted in me continually appealing their decision until they caved, they just told me that our city "didn't have cable." This was a daring move on their part because we did not live in the boondocks. Our hometown of Garden Grove, California had a population of 170,000 and was walking distance to Disneyland, the entertainment hub of the western hemisphere. I was supposed to believe our city built Disney*land* but couldn't figure out how to get the Disney *Channel*? But here's the thing: I *did* believe it. And much to my parents' surprise, I'm sure, I never asked about it again. Years later, we moved to a city where we were required to get cable and I rejoiced that we *finally* lived in a town with access to all the extra channels. I imagine my parents shared a silent nod of pride knowing they had saved thousands of dollars with this charade, and all they had to do was lie to their dumbest son.

LIE #7: THE BAND-AID FAIRY

Okay, here's the big one. Band-Aids are a paradox for kids. On one hand they believe these strips of plastic have supernatural healing powers on par with the Holy Grail. Whenever they scrape their knee, a Band-Aid must be applied immediately or they run the risk of bleeding out right there on the playground. However, once that bandage is placed on them, a ticking clock is set, counting down the seconds to the fateful moment it will be detached from their body with searing agony. Even getting

your kids to *consider* removing a Band-Aid takes a massive amount of bargaining. Instead of allowing you to spend one tenth of one second taking it off, kids would rather let their Band-Aid give them a nasty contact rash, slowly deteriorate over the course of many years, then turn into a fine powder that blows away in a gust of wind.

I now actually get mad when nurses put Band-Aids on my kids' arms. As if getting them a shot wasn't already a multiday anxiety circus for the whole family, the nurse follows it up by covering a microscopic wound with something my children consider to be a medieval torture device? But I've come up with a lie to avoid this quagmire altogether. Her name is the Band-Aid Fairy, and I have a feeling she'll be visiting your home very soon.

Tell your kid that if they want their bandage painlessly removed, all they have to do is wear short-sleeved jammies to bed. The Band-Aid Fairy will then fly into their room while they're snoozin', wave her wand, and when they wake up it'll be gone, just like magic! And here's all you have to do as the parent: Once your kid is in a deep sleep, you tiptoe in, grab the Band-Aid, and rip it right the fuck off.

In the beginning you'll feel like you're dismantling a bomb, but speed is key here. The first time I attempted this charade I took the Band-Aid off slowly because I was worried the sudden movement would wake up my daughter, but the prolonged peel nearly blew my cover. You must treat this like you're robbing a casino in an *Ocean's Eleven* movie: Get in and get out before they even know you were there (and if possible, make George Clooney do it).

This ploy is not only effective, it's scalable. If there are other grooming practices your child refuses to engage in, you can create spin-off characters to take care of those too. Say there's also a Floss Fairy, a Hairbrush Gnome, a Toenail-Trimming Elf…Assemble an entire Avengers-style team of hygiene pixies who make your kid slightly less gross while they sleep.

Call upon the Band-Aid Fairy. She's ready to serve. Almost as ready as you are to not have a dirty Buzz Lightyear bandage ruin your whole September.

Jesus said, "The truth will set you free," but you know what Jesus wasn't? A parent. A parent who always had kids trying to tickle his damn feet. So while I know lying to your kids doesn't feel right, it does feel *great*—and every time you do it you'll feel that immense pressure on your shoulders ease just a little bit. Plus if you're really good at lying, your kids won't realize you did it until they're adults, at which point this will all be their therapist's problem.

THE NO-FRIEND ZONE

One thing you are not prepared for when you have kids is what an unappetizing hang you will become. You convince yourself you can still be a cool person who just happens to carry around a satchel full of breast milk and cracker crumbs, but then suddenly you're at a Super Bowl party telling a *hilarious* story about the color of your baby's barf and realize you're now a professional-grade buzzkill. This change does not go unnoticed by your childless friends and, socially speaking, they will put you out to pasture like a cow with a broken leg.

This process is gradual. At first you still get invites just as you always have, but you either can't go because of your grueling new responsibilities, or you *do* go and disgust everyone at the barbecue by changing a diaper on the picnic table because "It's just pee!" Next you start receiving the halfhearted invite. Your friends feel bad your life is over, so they extend offers they know you could never possibly accept. "Hey, I don't know if babies are allowed there, but do you want to go see Metallica play in an abandoned rock quarry?"

Then the invites stop altogether. You hear secondhand about events you previously would have been invited to, and mutter phrases to yourself like "Who needs Mardi Gras when you've got peekaboo and pureed zucchini?!" Your friends now think you're as exciting as a cup of unflavored yogurt, and they are correct. The areas of your brain that used to secrete intrigue and charisma have been replaced with ones that store encyclopedic knowledge of which dogs drive which cars on *PAW Patrol*.

So here you are, weeping at a puppet show with a larval-stage human strapped to your chest. But all hope is not lost. While your options for companionship are now quite limited, there are still a few places you can find it if you're willing to lower your criteria for what you consider a "companion" (just like in *Cast Away* when Tom Hanks started dating that volleyball). Let's find you some force-a-friends!

AMAZON DELIVERY BESTIE

Whenever you're feeling lonely, order a box of Arm & Hammer baking soda on Amazon Prime. It has free one-day shipping and costs just $1.49, a small price to pay to summon your new soulmate. When you see the delivery driver approaching your mailbox, leap out of the bushes you've been waiting in all day and shout, "WOW PERFECT TIMING I AM ALSO ON THE PORCH!" To calm their racing pulse from this jump scare, offer the driver some sweet tea and tell them every single detail about your day until they back slowly into their doorless van and speed away. If you're one of those tree huggers who's worried about the environmental impact of a box truck driving to your home every time you're horny for small talk, just process a return for the previous day's baking soda and hand it to your delivery buddy when they bring you the new one. It'll be like you're exchanging gifts for the holidays, just like real friends do!

HIKERS WHO FALL DOWN YOUR OLD WISHIN' WELL

There's nothing a tired hiker likes more than a cool drink of water from a quaint 1800s wishing well. That's why you're going to build one in the woods near your home, and make a

few strategically placed bricks just a *little* too loose. Each Sunday morning, you can stroll up there and meet the new best friend who's fallen into your literal thirst trap (although for legal reasons, maybe don't call it a "trap"). Since you're the only human contact they will have had for the past thirty-six hours, they'll be *very* excited to make your acquaintance, and you'll both share a hearty laugh every time you send down a basket of lotion and do your famous impression of Buffalo Bill from *Silence of the Lambs*. If your well buddy happens to climb their way out and make it back into town, don't panic. That just means squad cars *filled* with new friends are racing to your home to tackle you—which is like a hug on the ground!

KIDS AT THE ZOO (NOTE: RISKY!)

Admittedly this involves some tact. Now that you have kids of your own, you've become quite good at chatting to younglings because you understand their interests and have a lot in common with them. "You can't tie your shoes? I tie someone's shoes *every day!*" Kids are also great conversationalists because they are literally incapable of not talking. So if you're at the zoo and a random kid blurts out unsolicited autobiographical info like "My name is Skyler and my pet lizard was named Donatello but we forgot to feed him flies one day so he died and then we buried him in our backyard but instead of a coffin we used an old box of Daddy's favorite drink which is called Mike's Hard Lemonade!!!"—feel free to engage. But exercise caution: You can only talk to a kid who's not yours for a maximum of one minute before security gets involved and you are permanently banned from the chimp enclosure.

DESPERATE HOME DEPOT SHOPPERS

Are you familiar with Home Depot, the dog park for dads? A common complaint about this establishment is that there are never enough employees walking around to answer questions for customers, but you are about to turn their chronic staffing issues into a friendship bonanza. All you need to do is buy yourself an orange smock and mosey down the aisles looking for guys holding one random screw. When you get flagged down by a stray father, examine the screw and say, "Wow, only professionals use these. If you need one, you must be working on *quite* a project. . . ." then settle in for the longest conversation of your life. You'll dig deep on such titillating topics as wood grain and linoleum flooring, and while you won't have any idea what this dude is talking about, doesn't it just feel nice to be wanted again? Every so often nod and say the name of a construction supply like "epoxy," and you'll be there till closing.

GRANDPA

Oh, he wishes you'd call more, huh? Well, it's time for that wrinkled racist to put his money where his dentures are. Place Pop-Pop on speed dial and start phoning him three times a day, letting him talk for hours on end about "the war" and how a loaf of bread only used to cost a buffalo nickel if you winked at the baker's daughter. It will take months, maybe even years, until he gets tired of hearing from you, so milk that lonely senior for every ounce of Ensure left in his brittle old bones. Let's make him regret he ever had a kid who had a kid who had a kid.

See? Your calendar is now *brimming* with social events that the other participants may or may not have agreed to. But hey, any port in a storm. And if all else fails, you can always "trip" down a *small* flight of stairs and wait for a Good Samaritan to come to your aid. They'll be talking your ear off in no time (mostly because they've heard you're not supposed to let a person with a concussion fall sleep), and when they ask you how many fingers they're holding up, say "Ronald Reagan." That gullible saint's not going anywhere.

OH, THE PLACES YOU WON'T GO

When you've been trudging through an extended period of infant-induced house arrest, you start to have crazy thoughts. Most are relatively harmless, like "My breakfast can be Starbursts" or "I'll cut my OWN bangs!!!" But there's one delusional notion we all flirt with and then immediately regret: "My kid and I should *go* somewhere."

Listen to me closely: Leaving the house with your children is a fool's game and you should avoid it unless absolutely necessary. If your kid has to go to the doctor or you are fleeing a volcanic eruption? Fine. Pack the diaper bag and run. But other than those two very specific circumstances, you must never take them anywhere if you want to stay sane. Particularly to the following locations:

THE PARK

The park *seems* like an easy outing with the children, but it is not—and this fallacy has caused the downfall of countless cocky parents. "What could my kid possibly need? She's going to go down the slide a few times, then eat some sand and catch the flu. No gear required." But the park is a hostile terrain where it's impossible to prepare for all possible scenarios.

First and foremost you must pack snacks—all the snacks you can pack in your sack. Then stuff all your pockets with them too, until you look like a human bodega. That's because kids at the park are like triathletes: They sprint around for hours expending every calorie of energy in their body, then slip into a hypoglycemic coma and can only be revived if you squirt a packet of orange goo in their mouth.

You also have to bring an extra outfit for each kid you're taking to the park, and I mean everything: backup shirt, pants, shoes, socks, hat, jacket, underwear, and backup backup underwear. At the park they can get soaking wet, covered in mud, sticky with ice cream, or coated in something far worse. During a park outing with our son when he was two, my wife and I watched him stumble over to a rock and start playing with it. It seemed like standard toddler stuff until we noticed he had been playing with it for an alarmingly long time, much longer than even the curiosity of a baby can be filled with a rock. We then discovered it was not actually a rock he was playing with, but a turd, which he was now covered in. And because we both shrieked, our son started crying. So we were now running around with a sobbing child covered in feces that were not his own, and it turns out they don't have washing machines or chemical showers at the playground.

Avoiding "The Park" also extends to all theme and amusement parks. If your kids are under forty-eight inches tall, rides are out of the question so you spend the entire day shuffling around in the sun, waiting in various lines to buy funnel cake and meet heatstroked adults dressed as Dora the Explorer.

And I know you *want* to do this, because taking your kid to an amusement park feels like a parenting rite of passage. But when they're young? *Everything* is amusing to them. They'd have just as much fun at home playing with an old boot, so going to a place with crowds and tickets and rules seems like a massive hassle to them. I discovered this when we took our daughter to Disneyland for her second birthday, and this is how that day *started*:

We basically drove two hours so our daughter could celebrate her special day by having a tantrum next to a log flume.

A couple years later we attempted to summit the Magic Kingdom again when our daughter was a little older and a little taller, assuming she'd have more fun this time because she could actually do stuff. This proved to be a much more difficult trip, however, because she *thought* she could do stuff, when in fact she could not.

This all came to a head at the Haunted Mansion. Even though I explained it was probably not the best place for little kids because it's a creepy old house filled with ghouls, she begged me to take her on it. And because my daughter has spoken like a manipulative adult since the day she was born, she knew all the right things to say:

"Daddy, I KNOW it's pretend."

"Daddy, I WON'T be scared."

"Daddy, it looks soooo FUN!"

I eventually relented, but realized I'd made a terrible mistake as soon as we walked into the ride's infamous "stretching room."

If you've never been in the Haunted Mansion, this part of the line is actually an elevator that takes you about twenty feet underground, but they use an optical illusion to make it look like the whole room is eerily stretching. During this, a "ghost host" tells you a number of spooky things, including the fact that "this chamber has no windows and no doors!" Upon hearing that, my daughter who "knew" this was all "pretend" scurried up my body with terror in her eyes and whispered, "We *need* to get *out* of here!" I told her it would be okay, and it *was* for the next one second—until the lights went out, there was a blood-curdling scream, and we saw the beloved kids' character "Dead Body Swinging from the Rafters."

I couldn't bear the thought of waiting in that long line for no reason, so I attempted to keep calm and carry on. But as I tried to load my daughter into a "Doom Buggy," she had her arms and legs stretched out like a cat avoiding the bath. I got a knowing glance from the ride operator, who pointed us toward the "Traumatized Child Escape Tunnel," and we emerged from the catacombs with a cherished memory and a lifetime of nightmares.

Even if you beat the odds and have a fantastical experience with your kids, every theme park visit ends with a specific phenomenon on the drive home. I don't care how sweet your child is on a daily basis or what a magical day they just had, once that car seat buckle clicks they embody the persona of a drunken *Real Housewife*: yelling, throwing punches, and saying shit they can never take back. One time after finishing a thirteen-hour day at Universal Studios, I strapped my kids in and, for literally no reason, one of them open-hand slapped the other one and they both started sobbing. It's as if spending that long at a theme park makes kids' dopamine receptors explode and get clogged up with churro dust, turning them into creatures that are neither man nor beast. So save yourself the hassle, the cost, and the mental anguish: no parks, themed or otherwise.

RESTAURANTS

Going to a restaurant with young kids requires the same amount of planning as a three-month backpacking trip through Cambodia. You need water, books, bibs, tiny cutlery, hand wipes, face wipes, ass wipes, and even though you're going to a place where your sole purpose is to eat food, you must bring a full meal your child will eat before, after, and *during* their purchased meal.

Those additional rations come in handy though, because when you get to the restaurant there's always a wait. And that's because any establishment willing to serve you and your two Garbage Pail Kids is not fancy enough to have a reservation system. No joke, my wife and I once showed up to a restaurant with our one-year-old, the hostess told us it was going to be a five-minute wait, and we just got back in our car and drove home. We knew we wouldn't survive.

If you do get seated, there's a critical moment that happens next: You meet your server, and this person lets you know if you're about to have a good time or a bad time. That's because the success of your meal hinges entirely on the waiter's understanding of the precarious position you find yourself in.

Servers who have kids themselves give you a booth without even asking, and before your butt hits the seat they've air-dropped you a massive basket of bread. That's your best-case scenario. But you know you're in trouble when the waiter starts asking lots of questions like "Have you dined with us before?" and "Would you like to hear the specials?" We would not, because this is kind of a triage situation and it's going to be best for everyone in this restaurant if some mini corn dogs appear on this table in the next three seconds.

The other thing many servers do is bring the kids' food out first "because it was ready." Pull this move and watch the hearts of every parent at the table sink into oblivion, because they know the kids are going to plow through their dinners and finish eating *just* as the grown-up food arrives. This forces the parents to eat in shifts, while the other parent walks the kids around the restaurant trying to keep them from touching strangers' entrées. If you are a waiter who drops off kid food before the parent food, the only moral thing to do is offer to babysit the children once they're done eating. That's just a great idea in general. I guarantee a restaurant that offered mid-meal babysitting would be the most popular restaurant in the world.

Just like with Olympic pommel horse, the trickiest part of dining out with kids is the dismount. Once you and your children have finished eating but are waiting for the check, you are under a form of culinary house arrest. Your kids are bored and whining. You're not feeling great because you shotgunned a plate of fajitas to get the meal done as fast as possible, but you can't leave. While the waiter casually prints the bill, *you* have to stop the property damage being done by your little wrecking crew who just split a gallon of fruit punch. But here's the second great idea I'm going to give all you restaurateurs out there: You know how when you stay at a hotel, instead of checking out at the front desk, you can just leave? Restaurants need this feature for parents. They take our credit card number up top, put a hold on it for incidentals, and then the second that last chicken finger gets crammed in our kid's mouth we vanish into the night like SEAL Team 6.

I know you're tired of cooking meals, but the amount of convenience you'll get from having an underpaid teenager make you a wedge salad will never outweigh the pain and suffering your children will cause you and the entire staff at this P. F. Chang's. Don't stress out, dine in!

VACATION

What's that, you need a *break*? And you think taking the kids on a getaway is going to rejuvenate you and the whole family? Have you learned *nothing* from this book? Just let me break down the realities of traveling with children, because you really only have four options:

- ✳ Go camping (nope)
- ✳ Stay with relatives (bigger nope)
- ✳ Rent a hotel room, where you pay $400 a night for your family to share a queen-size bedbug farm next to a broken ice machine
- ✓ Or get an Airbnb, which is really your only good choice ("good" being a relative term here)

Okay, so now you're in an Airbnb. This was clearly not a home designed with kids in mind, so you had to bring an SUV full of toys, games, tablets, blankets, baby swings, and high chairs. It now looks like your house vomited into a slightly nicer house. And if you think your kids don't respect *your* home, just wait until they're unleashed into a vacation rental owned by a random retired couple. Bob and Mitzy (there's no way they're not named Bob and Mitzy) spent their whole careers scrimping and saving to buy this little getaway and decorate it just right, and your kids are about to treat it like the Sex Pistols would a Ramada Inn: jumping off couches, body-slamming lamps, and urinating in the mini fridge. Suddenly what was supposed to be a relaxing weekend turns into forty-eight hours of chasing your kids around as they chip away at your security deposit.

As the saying goes, there is no "vacation" with children. Calling it a vacation implies it will include at least one moment where you and your spouse wear bathrobes on a balcony while steel drum music plays in the distance. When your kids come along, it's a "trip," which is what you take when you fly cross-country to visit your grandma in a retirement home. A "trip" is also what Grandma did down the stairs to put her *in* that retirement home, and you're going to feel just like her after you get off a six-hour flight with your infant.

My wife and I traveled to Hawai'i twice in the span of five years. The first time was right before we had kids, which was a vacation. The second time was with a four-year-old and a ten-month-old. That was a trip. Let me show you the difference:

On the left you see a twenty-nine-year-old boy with nothing on his agenda but getting drunk with his wife in an ill-advised vacation fedora. On the right is a thirty-four-year-old senior citizen who hasn't slept in a week, pining for the calm embrace of an overly long work meeting and a pile of spreadsheets.

On the way home from that trip, we were both emotionally and physically burnt, but convinced ourselves that at least our daughter had a great time. She swam, made friends with a ranch puppy, and rode a freaking horse! And yet six months later when we mentioned this to her, she had *zero* recollection of what we were talking about. She didn't know what Hawai'i was, and even claimed she had never ridden a horse. When I showed her the nine-hundred-picture photo spread I took of her on that horse, she said, "Huh. Looks like it was fun." It was. Expensive too!

So when your kids are along, don't vacation. Don't even staycation. Just . . . *stay*.

Look, I'm not trying to tell you how to live your life, but I am telling you to live it *exclusively* indoors. Sure, it'll be boring. But you *also* won't have to give your child a time-out at SeaWorld. So barricade the windows and lock the doors—it's time to start your fabulous new life as a voluntary agoraphobic!

NO-THRILL CHILL

The brain of a parent is like an old laptop: so overwhelmed with tasks that the little fan inside never stops spinning, and if you don't shut it down once a year it'll catch on fire. Sadly, standard forms of relaxation are not currently available to you, so much so that you've come to loathe people who *do* have time to unwind. But before you drive your RAV4 through the front of a Burke Williams, take a breath and read this chapter. We're going to turn over every stone to find you a few non-traditional roads to peace.

WALMART-A-LAGO

Some of the most soothing time parents get is when we have the immense *honor* of running an errand alone. You can only be away from home for a half hour before your kids feel abandoned and your partner files for divorce in a fit of envy, but that's plenty of time to squeeze in the parental equivalent of an island getaway at America's pool filter: Walmart. This is a store—nay, an *experience*, brimming with every leisure prod-uct imaginable and the most unsettling shoppers your community has to offer.

Grab a camping chair, a beach outfit you have no intention of purchasing, and kick back with a room-temp wine cooler next to their Great Wall of Vizio TVs. Yes, you are breaking a number of rules, but the employees will rush right by you to deal with much more pressing customer-relation issues, like the guy who's wearing nothing but Crocs pleasuring himself in the dog food aisle.

GO TO CHUCK E. CHEESE AND WATCH OTHER PEOPLE'S KIDS LOSE THEIR SHIT

The Germans have a word called *schadenfreude.* It's that sick euphoria you experience when the car in front of you gets into a horrible accident but you're completely unscathed. You see your fellow man suffering and think about how much it *rocks* to not be *them.* Well, there's an authentic Italian ristorante/video arcade where parents can soak up that amazing sensation day and night. The good Lord named it Chuck E. Cheese, and I recommend heading down there alone to gaze upon *dozens* of children who don't belong to you suffering pepperoni-fueled psychosis next to a Whac-A-Mole. The Mountain Dew blasting through their digestive tracts will cause these kids to commit a number of unspeakable acts, but you'll feel a sense of calm knowing every time you hear the phrase "Mom! He bit the rat!" the word "Mom" will refer to someone who is totally *not* you. This will leave you free to lean there with a latte and a warm smile on your face, basking in the glow of Skee-Ball tantrums that aren't remotely your problem (until the manager asks you to leave because you are "giving off major child abduction vibes").

(ANGRY) BIRD-WATCHING

Bird-watching is a leisure activity that's similar to being a Peeping Tom but even creepier. Grown adults walk around just lookin' in trees until they see a bird, and then tell other grown adults stuff like "Hey guess what? I saw a bird." They call this "birding," a name they maybe should have spent a few more minutes on. Despite its deeply dorky nature, birding is a good way to convene with nature, but since you're not allowed to go outside without dragging all your offspring around in a wagon, we'll need an indoor alternative. Luckily this can be achieved if you buy yourself a pair of binoculars and hide behind a houseplant in a corner of the living room. When you hear one of your kids fire up *Angry Birds* on the iPad, silently watch the screen from afar, marveling at the beautiful feather bouquet of "the red one" and knowing this still isn't as sad as what actual birders do.

NOISE BATH

Sound baths are a meditative process (often done in Los Angeles by nutty old white women) where you surround yourself with a sea of relaxing tones and get "bathed" in the sound. *You* don't have the luxury of engaging in such one-percenter pseudoscience, but you can re-create a similar experience at home in your child's play area. Go into their toy bins and dump out everything that makes an annoying noise: remote-control cars, robot dinosaurs, old greeting cards that sing "Jingle Bells" . . . Arrange these items in a sacrificial circle around you on the floor, then quickly press all 150 "on" switches. In the beginning this will be quite grating, and you'll only be able to focus on that one Ninja Turtle yelling "Cowabunga!" just a *little* too loud. But as more and more irritating noises join the symphony, they'll blend into an amalgam of beeps and dings that sounds like a thousand Toys "R" Us'es screaming out in beautiful agony. Let this digital cacophony wash over you, and absorb the energy of hundreds of AAA batteries into your own depleted soul.

SHAME PILE

If you're too busy to even consider the substitute tranquilities discussed here, you're going to need to cram all your recreation into one high-intensity day of balls-to-the-wall chilling I call the "Shame Pile." This is similar to the horror movie *The Purge* where all crime is legalized for twelve hours a year, except in this version you'll be committing crimes against your own body. Set this date on your calendar far in advance so you have something to look forward to. When it arrives, drop your kids off with a sitter, close the blinds, get as naked as the day you were born—then just eat, chug, puff, and tug anything that pops into your degenerate little mind. There are no rules on this day. Guilt and humiliation bounce off you like bullets off Superman. You want to eat a Filet-O-Fish off your bare gut and wash it down with an eighty-dollar bottle of Scotch? Do it. You want to watch *Shrek* and have a good cry? DO IT. You'll hit a wall after about four hours but *push through*. This is the same idea behind your dad making you suck down an entire carton of Marlboros to turn you off to smoking. You're going to relax so hard that even the thought of doing it again before a whole year has passed will make you sick to your stomach. At the end of the day, emerge from your

Debauchery Dungeon as if nothing happened. When the kids ask why the couch smells like ass and honey mustard, tell them that's a secret between you and the couch.

As they say, repose is in the eye of the beholder. Well, no one actually says that. Mostly because it's not true. But it *can* be true if you come to terms with your dire reality. And let's be honest, you didn't actually want to go on a tropical cruise anyway. Not only are they expensive, studies show they're the #1 place to catch fatal diarrhea from a seafood tower. (Note to editor: No need to fact-check that. Feels true.)

THE "CATEGORY FOUR"

Most of this section has been about measures of prevention, avoidance, and substitution, but another big part of preserving your mental health during your children's formative years is *acceptance*. While some catastrophes can be mitigated, others must be endured—none more so than an occurrence I've dubbed the "Category Four."

A lot of attention is given to children's "terrible two" and "threenager" periods, but the Category Four is an acute behavioral anomaly where at the age of four, every kid has a tantrum so unhinged and insane that their parents will remember it until the end of time.

There is no scientific data on what triggers a child's Category Four. Hunger? Sleep deprivation? A mummy's curse? It's likely some combination of the three. Just know that you will not recognize your child during this episode, for they will mutate into something truly wicked. Your sweet baby, who usually loves snuggles and songs and butterfly kisses, will say the meanest shit you've ever heard then kick you square in the throat.

This is a moment in which the wheels come off and all perception of your authority evaporates. You will be terrified, and your instinct will be to step in and stop the havoc. But you cannot parent your way out of a Category Four. Your only option is to let your body go limp and get bashed against the rocks.

That's because for your kid, this event will come and go like a passing tide. But if you try to contain it, you'll only increase the blast radius. Stoicism is key when a Category

Four is bearing down on you, and to prove it I'm going to tell you about both times I screwed that up.

STORM 1: AUGUST 21, 2017 (DAUGHTER)

Our daughter's C4 came just five days after the birth of her brother. She was, admittedly, going through a lot. In her mind she had carved out an ideal existence for herself: three blissful years as the center of our only-child universe. She had 100 percent of our attention, didn't have to share a single toy, and was the first grandkid in our family, which meant she had Kylie Jenner status: famous and beloved simply for existing. But then a human meat loaf came blasting out of her mother and threatened her very way of life.

Our daughter's first few days as a big sister were tenuous at best. One moment she'd help by feeding her new sibling a bottle, the next she'd politely suggest that things might be better if we "put brother in a dumpster." But on this day we had to take our son to the doctor for his first pediatrician checkup, and on the drive back the weight of the week caught up with her all at once. As we pulled into the driveway she randomly started wailing, then threw herself on the ground and writhed around like she was caught in a bear trap. She kept refusing to come inside, and as I carried her into the house she began kicking me in the head like a little Jackie Chan.

She was clearly not in her right mind, and if I'd just given her milk and half a graham cracker this probably would have ended quickly—but kicking your dad in the head seemed like a punishable offense, so I put her in a time-out. Unfortunately, the only thing that accomplished was drawing this out by a factor of ten. She kept leaving the corner as an act of uncivil disobedience, so to keep her in place I had to stand there like a prison guard while she bellowed and thrashed as if she'd been possessed by Garashkar the Tantrum Beast. Her voice got guttural, her screams became blood-curdling. I would not have been surprised if she'd hissed at me, bent over backward, and scurried up the wall like a scorpion. Also, I don't know if this was related, but at that exact moment there was a solar eclipse happening (the one Donald Trump stared directly into with his big strong eyes), and it turns out that's the scariest possible setting for a preschool exorcism.

Eventually, we came to a détente when my daughter had raged so hard she fell dead asleep with her head against the wall, dangerously close to an electrical socket.

When she regained consciousness, she remembered absolutely none of it. And yet, I will relive this moment in vivid color until the day I die.

STORM 2: OCTOBER 10, 2021 (SON)

My second Category Four led to perhaps my most embarrassing moment as a parent. I should have just let the squall ride itself out, but I didn't, and it ended up costing me forty-nine dollars (plus tax).

Even though our son is the sweetest soul I have ever known, at age four he went through a phase where he'd take radical stances on completely nonsensical issues. He would aggressively refuse to put on his socks, or yell at us for serving him chicken nuggets he had literally just asked for. After six months of this my wife and I would become instantly triggered by it, and arguments would escalate quickly over things like him insisting on taking a teddy bear in the shower.

On this day, our son had used the hose to make a puddle in the backyard and was dunking an entire roll of paper towels into it. I asked him—quite calmly, I might add—to stop doing this. But he, also quite calmly, said no. I again asked him to stop, and he again declined, loudly this time to make sure I heard it. I told him if he didn't knock it off by the time I counted to three he'd get a time-out, but he defiantly went right back to dipping the towels, like a little Braveheart in Hulk underwear. So I counted, and as the word "three!" rang out over the yard, we locked eyes and a deafening silence set in. We were calling each other's bluff.

He refused to peacefully surrender for his time-out, so like a cop detaining a perp on bath salts, I carried my son away while he screamed and struck me in all my softest tissues. When I finally got him to his room we were both panting and sweating, so I left him alone to reflect on how badly he'd just treated his own father. But literally one second later I heard him happily playing and singing as if nothing had happened.

Now here is where we get into my biggest weakness as a parent: I always need to make a point. To teach a life lesson. To make each punishment a touchstone moment in my child's life that they will look back upon decades from now and think, "Dad was tough but fair, and that's why I'm now the president of the United States." There have been many behavioral conflicts where if I'd just been cool and let things slide, all emotion would have dissipated on both sides and we instantly would have been back to normal. But I'm always worried that if my kids get away with assholish behavior as children, they will grow up to be assholish adults who sit in their cars texting while someone waits for their parking spot, and that I cannot permit.

So this is when I made a choice that was both right *and* bad. Because my son was exhibiting a complete lack of remorse for what he'd done, I barged back into his room with the vague punishment goal of "not letting him have fun" for some undetermined amount of time. With immense frustration in my voice I asked, "What's your favorite toy?" He didn't answer, so I grabbed his *PAW Patrol* Mighty Lookout Tower, took it out of his room, and put it on the porch. I honestly don't know why I grabbed the tower. Perhaps I thought lifting something shaped like a building would make me seem like an intimidating King Kong–like creature worthy of respect? And I put it on the porch because . . . I have no idea. This was punishment jazz.

And yes, I know this is not a good look for me. I was now acting more childish than the child I was trying to discipline, but I was too frenzied to realize it. Since my son had no reaction to my ridiculous showing on the porch, and I was determined to make him feel one iota of contrition, I led him out of his room and put him in the time-out corner (the same one my daughter passed out in during her Category Four. That piece of drywall has seen some *shit*). I told him to face the corner, because that seemed like it would be more "punish-y," but he screamed "No!". I turned him toward the wall, he turned back, over and over again. I saw I was outgunned here, so I carried him back to his room to give him a stern talking-to (my heart rate was now so high my Fitbit thought I was rowing a canoe). I then asked him to look me in the eye while I reprimanded him, but he wouldn't. And in an act of contempt, he turned to face the wall (*now* he faces the wall!).

This was another point when I should have just walked away and let this whole thing be over, but then my son would have won our very stupid standoff and I was afraid that would send a litany of wrong messages. My mind was racing, my blood pressure was through the roof, and I had run out of ways to get his attention, so in a moment of immense exasperation I slammed my hand down on the top of his Ikea bookcase. Unfortunately, the extra adrenaline in my hand combined with Ikea's relentless commitment to particleboard furniture caused something I did not intend or anticipate: I *obliterated* this thing. I mean completely destroyed the top shelf of it, like those videos of Steven Seagal chopping boards at a karate demonstration.

Now, this moment was a real mixed bag for me because first and foremost I was immensely ashamed. I had let my anger get the best of me, and I lost control of my emotions in front of my young son. On the other hand, this was the one and only show of physical strength I've ever exhibited in my entire life and I *kinda* wish I had slo-mo video of it. Thankfully my son didn't see it (he was facing the wall, after all), and when we finally had our talk, we hugged each other and agreed to handle things more calmly next time. He then asked, "What happened to my bookshelf?" and I had to tell him the uncomfortable truth: "I think your mom broke it."

I learned something very important that day: You can't fight a fight. And when I tried to do so, my son's Category Four led to me having my own Category *Thirty-Four*. So when your child's inevitable C4 begins to swell, keep a few things in mind.

(1) THIS IS NOT ABOUT YOU

It's easy to take everything your kids do personally, but you must view children like internet commenters: irrational lunatics with soft spots on their skulls. If a respected coworker started kicking you in the gut while wearing just a diaper, okay yeah—might be worth trying to figure out why she did that. But there's nothing you did to cause a Category Four, and you'll never know the reason it happened, because there *is* no reason it happened. Just like how Keith Richards is still alive, it's okay for some things in life to remain a mystery.

(2) THIS IS NOT ABOUT THEM

It's hard to believe, but when your child is in this state of temporary derangement trying to bite off your thumbs, it is not indicative of who they are as a person. I bet even a toddler Paul Rudd once had a freak-out so bad he ruined brunch for everyone at an IHOP. There is no behavior to correct here, so don't even try. This is not a time to lecture. It is a time to cower.

(3) THERE'S NOTHING YOU CAN DO TO STOP THIS

You wouldn't go outside during a hurricane and try to wrestle the wind, so don't make the same mistake here. No amount of reasoning will cool your child's head, no punishment will quell this emotional monsoon. Like with any natural disaster, your only choice is to hide in the cellar and let this cyclone run its course (until it falls asleep with its head on a light socket).

ERADICATE ALL MAGICAL
HOLIDAY CREATURES

As we near the end of our quest to save your time, money, and mind, I have one final pitch that's going to bring all three of them together in glorious fashion. It is both radical and controversial, but if we work together to pull this off, it will give us back more of our lives than all the other advice in this book combined. It may even change the face of parenting for generations to come. Are you ready?

We're going to kill the Easter Bunny. And all his little friends too. Which . . . I know. But let me lay out my case.

Before we were parents, we looked forward to someday celebrating the holidays with our kids, pretending our homes were being visited by mythical beings who bring the little ones gifts and joy. The idea of getting to participate in these cherished stories with our own families just sounded like good, wholesome fun, and a chance to feel like part of something bigger than ourselves.

But in reality, this whole process is a living nightmare for us. A full-time unpaid job. We assumed these traditions were in perpetual motion—that they just *happen* because they've *always* happened. But we were wrong. These magical holiday creatures only exist because our parents worked their asses off to maintain them, and now we've gotta work ours off too. For the next twenty or so years, *we* are the stewards of these unfathomably silly burdens. Unless—and hear me out—we just . . . stop.

These jolly assholes are robbing us of our time, money,

and minds—so let's band together and collectively send them to the great beyond. Here's our hit list:

SANTA

The most obvious magical being for us to eliminate is the gluttonous showboater known as Santa Claus. I don't mean to sound harsh but FUCK this guy. You save money all year. You spend months buying your kids presents. You stay up all night on Christmas Eve stuffing candy into socks and assembling dollhouses with a tiny little wrench. And then you're supposed to give all the credit to this home invader in a fur-lined pimp suit? No way. Fuck that. You wouldn't spend three hours making a meal from scratch, then tell your kids, "The Dinner Fairy left this for you!" No, bro. *I* made the linguine. Clap for *me*. Have you ever worked a job where you have a bunch of great ideas, do a bunch of work, and then your old, white boss takes all the glory? *That* is Santa! And the harder we work at lifting Santa up, the worse *we* seem to our kids. "Santa got me a swing set and you got me a humidifier? Why do you love me less than the strange man who lives at the mall?" Also Santa is *fuckin'* weird, dude. Let's say in, like, August, you met a bearded man walking down the street chuggin' a glass of milk and holding a scroll of kids' names he calls the "Naughty List".... Would you say, "Hey, sneak into my house at midnight and eat some cookies off the hearth"? No, you'd call the FBI!

And lastly...look, my lawyers have advised me not to lodge serious accusations here, but I will just say I have a lot of Jewish friends, and Santa always seems to "forget" to bring them gifts. Really think about that one for a second. We are all in a toxic relationship with this cherry-cheeked anti-Semite (allegedly!) and we need to cut him out of our lives. Next up . . .

THE TOOTH FAIRY

An oral hygiene imp fraught with issues. She's not even tied to a holiday but I'm lumping her in. This is a woman who hears through some kind of seedy underground back channel that a six-year-old has lost a tooth and enters their room while they're sleeping (another home invader!). She then leaves a crumpled dollar bill under the child's pillow and takes the tooth for her collection. Ask yourself, did I just explain a beloved childhood tradition or a season of *True Detective*?

The Tooth Fairy myth also requires a lot of disgusting back-end work for the parents. People often say changing diapers is the nastiest part of having kids, but I think it's handling their hollow little rat teeth. And what are you supposed to do with all those teeth once you have them? Throwing them in the trash feels cruel because it's a piece of your child, but there's really no good place to put them. I personally have a metal tin in the back of my sock drawer filled with dozens of baby teeth, which sounds like a tidbit you'd read in a biography about Jeffrey Dahmer. And I have no idea what my endgame is here. On my kids' eighteenth birthdays do I tearfully give them back their old teeth while blubbering, "You used to chew string cheese with these"?

Plus, the financial implications of the Tooth Fairy are concerning, to say the least. First of all, it's hard enough to get kids to brush their teeth, and now this maniac is giving them a monetary incentive not to do so? And in a ruthless act of capitalism, the Tooth Fairy pays more money for the teeth of wealthy children. (Maybe they go for more on the dark web chat rooms she sells them on???) This becomes a big issue once your kid and their friends all start losing teeth, because they compare dental salaries and things get messy. Your child might get twenty-five cents a tooth, but their friend with the stockbroker parent is getting fifty bucks a pop. This is some class warfare bullshit and when Bernie Sanders finds out about it, he's gonna jab his finger in the air so hard he'll fly to the moon. Just like how we need a national minimum wage, we need a federally mandated amount the Tooth Fairy is allowed to pay per incisor. Or, perhaps, we could all just tell our kids that the Tooth Fairy passed away. Nothing tragic. Let's just agree that she lived long ago and died heroically fighting alongside George Washington in the Revolutionary War, cool?

THE AMCs (AUXILIARY MAGICAL CREATURES)

I have noticed a growing trend that is both inexplicable and inexcusable: parents creating their own next-generation holiday creatures where they did not exist before. What the fuck with this? I don't care how cute you think it is—you *cannot* be inventing new characters to visit your home, because kids talk and word will get out.

It's for the same reason you're not allowed to bring non-indigenous animals to an island: They'll spread like wildfire and infect the entire nation. One year *you* set up a funny little scene that makes it look like your turkey tried to escape the night before Thanksgiving, and then a year later *every parent at your school* is up late on Thanksgive Eve making fake turkey footprints with cranberry sauce.

I've heard of parents orchestrating cupid visits for

Valentine's, or even staging a whole scene on Saint Patrick's Day, complete with pots of gold and leprechaun traps. Did these people grow up under power lines? February and March are a beautiful gift-free holiday reprieve between Christmas and Easter. We're cramming in another decorate-the-house-at-midnight Black Ops mission no one was asking for? Plus as we all know, Saint Patrick's Day is a thinly veiled excuse to get drunk while culturally appropriating the Irish. We don't need to drag the children into this.

I blame this whole phenomenon on the Elf on the Shelf, which I assumed had been invented in 1700s Norway or something. But nope! 2005. In America. By some rando lady. And look what happened! Her dumb family holiday tradition became a national headache. I don't know a single parent who doesn't want to cram that shelf up the ass of the elf by day two. It's twenty-four homework assignments in a row, and if you forget just *once*, your child no longer believes in magic. Sounds fun! And do your *kids* even like this? He's an informant who reports their bad behavior back to Santa. He's not an Elf on the Shelf. He's a Snitch in the Kitchen.

The other thing you need to consider is that if you successfully create a new holiday creature, your kids will lock you into a multiyear contract for it. I know this because even I, the world's least whimsical parent, got myself entangled with an Auxiliary Magical Creature.

Our daughter absolutely loves the Grinch, and when she was three she got worried he was going to come steal all her presents on Christmas Eve. Cute, right? So we told her to write the Grinch a note begging for mercy, and not only did he not steal her presents, he brought her a special gift! A banana peel and a Grinch book. It was so precious, until eleven and a half months later when she started bragging about all the stuff her buddy the Grinch was going to bring her that year. And that was on top of the stuff Santa was bringing her (they can't coordinate, obviously, for they are bitter rivals). So now, even seven years later, we're on the hook for both Santa gifts *and* Grinch gifts. We leave plates of cookies *and* onions on the mantle. I've bought pretty much every piece of illegally printed Grinch merch Etsy has to offer. At this point the only Christmas the Grinch steals is *mine.*

So if you're one of these parents trying to add additional characters to our collective national holiday canon? No one likes you. Cut the shit. And now let's dig into the most baffling, unnecessary, exasperating magical holiday creature of them all . . .

THE GODDAMN EASTER BUNNY

Hoo boy. Okay first off, the Easter Bunny is the most mentally taxing holiday creature for parents because he has the least defined backstory *by far*—which requires us to fill in a lot of details on the fly. My son once asked me where the Easter Bunny lives and I said, "I don't know, the dirt?" Then my daughter speculated the bunny gets around the whole world in one day by "riding on a stray cat," and we said sure, because that's just as plausible as any other part of his tragically under-written biography. My kids wanted to send the Easter Bunny a letter, but . . . can he read? Can he write a response? Does he have hands that can hold a pen, or just paws? We don't even know what size he is. For real, poll your friends on this and you'll get a bunch of radically different responses. Could be a regular-size rabbit, could be a seven-foot beast with erect bipedal mobility. *We have no idea.* We also don't know *why* the Easter Bunny does what he does. He doesn't bring you jelly beans because you were good. He's not buying your dead teeth. He just shows up and throws eggs on your lawn like a drunk Instacart driver. Also, this egotist leaves little chocolate versions of himself that our kids are supposed to *eat*? That is some sick and twisted shit right there. *Consume my vessel. I am hollow within.*

Plus, the Easter Bunny has zero real connection to the Easter holiday. Jesus did not have a pet rabbit. He did not rise from a plastic egg. In fact, I looked it up and this is true: According to the University of Florida's Center for Children's Literature and Culture, this whole bunny thing dates back to thirteenth-century Germany where they celebrated various deities on Easter, including Eostrae, the goddess of fertility. Her symbol was a rabbit because, and again, I am not making this up, rabbits are famous for their constant fucking. Eggs are also an ancient symbol of fertility for obvious reasons—so that fun little scavenger hunt you do with the kids? It's basically because a horny rabbit emptied its fallopian tubes all over your yard. And my lawyers have once again advised me against saying anything actionable here, but I'm just going to ask you a question: Have you ever seen a Jewish kid holding an Easter basket? Just throwing that out there.

So we need to eliminate this sexually aroused candy mammal from our lives, that much is clear. But short of that, we at least need to stop taking our kids to get a picture with him at the mall. Please. If there's one thing I accomplish with this book, I hope it's that. Visiting Santa kinda makes sense:

You need to ask him for stuff, but he's too old to use email so an in-person visit is required. However, why see the Easter Bunny? There's no conversation to be had because he only brings you one thing and OH YEAH, HE CANNOT SPEAK. So really all you're doing is paying fifty dollars to have your kids take a photo with a sad teenager dressed as a furry. And I know that because in the year 2000 at the Mission Viejo Mall in Mission Viejo, California . . . I was that sad teenager.

Me (costumed), my sister, Whitney (over-alled), and the moment the last shred of dignity left my body

Yes, I'm a little biased here, but it's time to end this lunacy. Let's get rid of all these fairy dust motherfuckers once and for all. Maybe *we* don't even have to do it; perhaps we can orchestrate some kind of intricate double-cross where they all kill each other off in a warehouse like the end of *Reservoir Dogs*. I know that's dark, but think about what this could mean!

No longer will we have to live this lie . . . sneaking around, taking single bites out of cookies, keeping up the illusion that elves have the technological know-how to build an Xbox. We can finally be ourselves, and all future parents will be free to be themselves too. Eons from now, historians will look back on this as the moment parents all over the world stood up and declared in one voice that we are stopping the cycle. That we're getting off the ride. That we're going to quit believing in fairies and Santas and erotic rabbits . . . and start believing in *ourselves*. Who's with me?!

. . . I hope all of you are, because if not I have to keep my creepy tin of baby teeth.

MILLION-DOLLAR IDEAS: MIND-SAVER EDITION

It's our last chance to make you millions! This final batch of inventions will preserve your mind and can be utilized when your children have grated your patience down to a fine Parmesan cheese–like substance.

THE PARENT PRIVACY PARTITION

Many limousines have a soundproof privacy window so the drivers can't hear their celebrity passengers doing cocaine and yelling at their publicists, but you know who *actually* needs one of those? Parents on long road trips with their kids (and really parents driving *anywhere* with their kids). When your children start a blood feud over the armrest during your all-day drive to Des Moines, just roll this baby up, hermetically seal your kids in the back, and listen to the podcast of your choice (or just enjoy a nice silent place to scream).

REASONABLE REQUEST LOOP MACHINE

They say the definition of insanity is doing the same thing over and over again and expecting a different result, which also happens to be the definition of parenting. Your entire day is spent repeating sentences like "Brush your teeth" and "You're petting the gerbil too hard," hoping that at least one of those requests will randomly break through to your children. But we can automate this process with the help of a device that revolutionized hip-hop: the 808 drum machine. These little boxes are usually used to loop beats, but we're going to program this one with the sound of your voice begging your kids to do everyday tasks. Just record yourself once, hit the repeat button, and don't turn it off until they've finally cleaned all those raisins out of the cable modem. And who knows, if you're lucky a clip of you asking your kid to wash their feet might get sampled by Kendrick Lamar and make you a *multi*millionaire!

THE SHENANIGAN SHACKLE

Over a hundred years ago, an innovative parenting tool was invented called the child safety harness. Okay sure, this was a leash for kids. But it allowed parents to prevent their little ones from running into traffic or being carried off by large birds, and remained quite popular until "experts" using "data" determined treating your child like a poodle could have "lasting psychological effects boo-hoo-hoo." Well, you know what's never caused lasting psychological effects? A good old-fashioned three-legged race. And with the Shenanigan Shackle your children will soon adopt it as a way of life. This is a strong military-grade nylon strap that binds your kids together at the ankle. Your children will be free to roam wherever they please, but to get far away from you they'll have to work together, and we know *that* ain't happening. You'll never lose sight of them again, plus they'll be impossible to kidnap. (It's much harder to steal a six-pack than a can.)

WEIGHTED DECORATIONS

A big source of agita for me is my children "redecorating" my home. My wife and I have curated an extensive collection of home goods to make our home feel good and home-y, but every time a new tchotchke enters the premises our kids take it upon themselves to find a "better" location for it: usually under their bed, inside the dishwasher, or up on the roof. But that will be a concern of the past with Weighted Decorations. This is a line of knickknacks and bric-a-bracs, each with a seventy-five-pound cast-iron weight built into the bottom. That way you know wherever you and your spouse place that candle, it's gonna stay right the fuck there. And if your child does eventually pick one of these up after months of trying, it's going to be because they're completely shredded now. That decorative bowl gave your baby some *pump*.

CYBERCOUCH

After many years of development, Tesla finally released their truly hilarious vehicle, the Cybertruck. This is an electric, angular, and (for some reason) bulletproof truck created exclusively for the micro-penis community. It's ridiculous, but it did give me an idea for something that will relieve a ton of parental stress: We need a Cybercouch. Like all red-blooded Americans I consider my couch a foam-filled sanctuary, but my kids consider it a trampoline/napkin. They seem hell-bent on sending our sectional to an early grave, but what if we could build a couch made from thick sheets of aluminum with a reinforced alloy exoskeleton? Your kids wouldn't be able to put a dent in that thing. And neither would Joe Rogan, who will be impulsively shooting a crossbow at it (for some reason).

Conclusion

WHY, HELLO THERE.

Look at you, Champ. You followed all my advice, and now you're relaxed, sexy, rich, and doing whatever the hell you want, which right now is lounging topless on a private island while playing hard-to-get with one of the hotter Hemsworth brothers. You've found the perfect balance between your parenting and personal lives and achieved a level of happiness that's both permanent and tantric.

End of book.

Actual Conclusion

Okay maybe not, but you *did* just finish a book for the first time this decade, which is definitely a step in the right direction.

Here's the lesson I hope you take away from all this: You're doing great as a parent. Actually, you're doing *too good* as a parent, and for your own sake you need to calm the fuck down. Dialing it back isn't shortchanging your kids; it's preserving a few critical resources for yourself. And doing so will allow you to be your own person *and* a great parent. Not because you spent your entire Labor Day watching your kid get ringworm at a water park, but because you'll have enough internal peace to be balanced, focused, and present with your children. Plus, the stuff you're wasting your time and money and mind on? That's not the stuff your kids will remember.

Now that I'm forty, when I look back at my childhood I don't have distinct memories of the times my parents tried really hard. I know they *did*, because they did a great job raising me and my siblings, but I have almost no memory of them Parenting with a capital *P*. All the times they took me to a theme park blend together into one vaguely amusing churro buffet. I can't tell you a single present Santa ever brought me. My most vivid memory from a family vacation isn't frolicking at some beach resort with my brother and sister. It's when my dad comforted me as I got violently seasick into a Wendy's bag.

Throughout my youth my parents poured countless hours and thousands of dollars into events and experiences they thought would be cherished moments for the rest of my life, but the joke's on them because the stuff that stuck with me—my actual favorite memories with them—are the ones they weren't expecting:

- My mom cleaning my pet parakeet's cage every week because even though I demanded to have one, I was terrified of birds.

- My dad pulling me up an icy mountain for three hours after I ignored his repeated requests to not go hiking in slip-on Vans.

- My mom starting a conversation with me in a mall food court with the sentence: "I want you to tell me if you're sexually active, and if you say no, I'll know you're lying."

- My parents beaming after an elementary school rendition of *The Sound of Music* where I played Maria's dog. You might be saying, "Maria doesn't have a dog in *The Sound of Music*," and you would be right.

- The way my 6'4" father sprints like Yogi Bear over to the rest of us after he sets the timer on a camera. It's why we're dying laughing in all our family photos.

- My (neonatal nurse) mom making me a "dad care package" when we were going to the hospital for the birth of our first child because "everyone forgets the father!" And my dad silently slipping this note into my backpack that day, written on a greeting card he bought in the gift shop downstairs:

Danny,
Today your life will change forever in
ways you can't begin to imagine.
All of your priorities will change and you will
never love anything more than your little girl.
She will become the reason for your greatest
concerns, and your greatest joy and pride.
You and Kelly are going to be great parents
and I know you are going to be a wonderful
father. I'm so proud of you both.
Love you,
Dad

That three minutes of effort and two dollars of card stock meant more to me than all my birthday parties combined. And that, I think, is the point here. The reason this random collection of moments made an impression on me isn't that they were expensive or time-consuming for my parents; it's because they were genuine acts of kindness, warmth, and humor. The types of moments you can't give your kids if you've pulled an all-nighter hot gluing *Bluey* party hats you found on Pinterest.

My dad once told me that your only real responsibility as a parent is to love your kids as hard as you can, and he's right. Everything else is cake fondant: flashy but absent of taste and nutrition.

So skip the PTA meeting. Hide in the attic if you want to watch Netflix. Let it slide when your kid says "fuck." Because while it feels like every corner you cut will alter the life path of your children, it won't. In fact, it can't. All you have to do is love them as hard as you can.

And tell them the Easter Bunny is dead.

ABOUT THE AUTHOR

DANNY RICKER is a father, husband, author, and Emmy-nominated writer-producer from Burbank, California. He has written for the Oscars, the Primetime Emmys, the White House Correspondents' Dinner, and currently serves as co-head writer and co-executive producer at *Jimmy Kimmel Live!*, where he has worked since he was a small baby.

DannyRicker.com
Instagram: @HeyDannyRicker
Bluesky: @DannyRicker.Bsky.Social
The Website Formerly Known as Twitter: @DannyRicker

ACKNOWLEDGMENTS

Writing a book is a lot of fucking work, and I never would have gotten here without the help of the following people. I would like to thank...

My guardian angel, Jimmy Kimmel. His kindness, advice, generosity, loyalty, and friendship mean more to me than my limited writing capabilities can put into words. He has taken many chances on me, given me all my big breaks, and America may never forgive him for that. As a thank you, I will continue not inviting him over to my house.

My mother, Cindy, who is as good as they come. She turned a difficult childhood for herself into an amazing one for her kids. I love her as much as she loves me (which is a lot, she tells me).

My father, John, who has always led by example when it comes to hard work, integrity, loving his family, and buying used jackets with prophylactics in the pocket.

My sister, Whitney, the funniest and most caring member of our family who binds us all together (and informed me I'd spelled "wiener" two different ways in this book).

My brother, Bryan, who will be mortified I'm mentioning him in a remotely emotional context, so I'm just gonna leave it there.

My in-laws, Jeff Kim, Leilenah Mamea, Lynn Crookes, and Kristen Crookes, who have made my already wonderful family even better.

Thomas Crookes, Wayne Ricker, and Kamell Allaway,

three great fathers we lost whose legacies live on through their kids, grandkids, and great-grandkids.

Josh Halloway, the Siegfried to my Roy. He read many versions of this book (including all the terrible ones) and gave me the right notes at the right time to make this what it is. Thank you for always being a great creative partner and an even better friend.

Jesse Joyce, the gentleman scholar. A fantastic writer and exemplary person who let me try out a lot of this material on him as we stomped around studio lots during the 2023 WGA strike.

Molly McNearney and Gary Greenberg, who went from being my bosses to my mentors to my partners to my very close friends. I'm lucky to have you both.

Nick DiLorenzo for fact-checking this book, and being the best online accountability partner a guy could ask for.

Bernd Reinhardt for taking my thirst trap author photo.

My entire *Jimmy Kimmel Live!* family for their unwavering humor, warmth, and vigor: our writers, writers' assistants, producers, crew, bookers, APs, PAs, stage managers, directors, editors, lawyers, segment department, integrations team, Sosh Meed Squad, hair and makeup artists, publicists, executives, prop builders, wardrobe designers, craft servers, graphic guys, the Cletones, and my nephew Guillermo.

Dan Bodansky for managing both my career and my anxiety about that career.

Dan Strone for getting this unknown author his first book deal.

James "Babydoll" Dixon for pushing me to make this book

something bigger than it was, and for showing me firsthand just how cool smoking can be.

My very patient and encouraging team at Hyperion Avenue: Jen Levesque, Elias Kotsis, Amy King, Daneen Goodwin, Kelly Forsythe, Guy Cunningham, Sara Liebling, Sylvia Davis, and Karen Krumpak.

The great Jon Kutt for his hilarious illustrations all throughout this book. (Enjoy his delightfully weird art at TheHighRoadDesign.com.)

The many wonderful teachers I've been blessed with in my life, especially Cheryl Des Palmes who pushed me to believe in myself when I did not know how to do that.

My friends who have kept me afloat all these years: Kyle and Allie Benham, Ruby and Mike Brown, Henry and Sarah Dittman, Bryan and Katie Green, Andy and Jeff Crocker, Adam Fisher, Whitney Timmons, Natasha Arnold, Kurt Scholler, Greg Beirne, Kina Grannis, Jesse Epstein, Nikos Karamigios, Amanda McCann, Greg Martin, Brad Mulcahy, Sal Iacono, Doug Karo, Mike Hughes, Phillip Wilburn, my therapist Dr. Canter, my ComedySportz family, my *Mike & Ben* family, and LA's Golden God Dallas Raines for always giving us the forecast and keepin' it tight.

My wife, Kelly Ricker, whom I would wither without. Thank you for your infinite support, for giving us two amazing children, and for not even questioning it many years ago when I had the ill-advised idea to become a comedy writer. Love you forever.

My son, the beating heart of our family, whose empathy and curiosity are infectious. You have taught me the meaning of unconditional love and the name of every dinosaur.

And finally my daughter, who made me a dad and enriches my life in countless ways. I confided in her recently that I was worried some people might not like my book, and we had this exchange:

Me: "I just keep trying to remind myself that you can't control what people think about you. . ."

Her: "But you *can* control what you think about *them*, and I think those people are garbage."

Thanks for always looking out for me, Cap. xo

If you'd like to ask Danny for completely unqualified advice (parenting or otherwise), email your questions to heydannyricker@gmail.com and he may answer your queries in future writings.